Sorting It Out

Written for parents, teachers, and others who live or work with teenagers, this science-based guide describes how you can become a confident "decision mentor." Learn to support young people in making good decisions for themselves. Treating decision making as an essential and learnable skill, the six-step "Decision-Maker Moves" highlight the power and promise of young people as they shape their lives through the options they choose. Stories, examples, and practical tips show how decisions can transform problems into opportunities. Each chapter provides common-sense advice on when and how to talk with teenagers as they weigh up the often-conflicting values, emotions, and trade-offs affecting their choices. We cannot provide young minds with all the answers, but we can help them as they navigate both life-changing and everyday decisions.

Robin Gregory is a parent and grandparent, Adjunct Professor at the University of British Columbia, and Senior Research Scientist at Decision Research, Oregon. He helps families, communities, and governments worldwide address difficult decisions involving diverse perspectives, uncertainty, and tough trade-offs in ways that reflect and help achieve their values.

Brooke Moore is a parent, Adjunct Professor at the University of British Columbia, and a District Principal in the Delta School District, British Columbia. Throughout these roles, both professional and personal, she is motivated by a vision where all young people can move into adulthood with dignity, purpose, and options, a phrase she learned through her work with the Network of Inquiry and Indigenous Education.

Sorting It Out

Supporting Teenage Decision Making

Robin Gregory

University of British Columbia and *Decision Research, Oregon*

Brooke Moore

University of British Columbia and *Delta School District, British Columbia*

CAMBRIDGE
UNIVERSITY PRESS

Shaftesbury Road, Cambridge CB2 8EA, United Kingdom

One Liberty Plaza, 20th Floor, New York, NY 10006, USA

477 Williamstown Road, Port Melbourne, VIC 3207, Australia

314–321, 3rd Floor, Plot 3, Splendor Forum, Jasola District Centre, New Delhi – 110025, India

103 Penang Road, #05–06/07, Visioncrest Commercial, Singapore 238467

Cambridge University Press is part of Cambridge University Press & Assessment, a department of the University of Cambridge.

We share the University's mission to contribute to society through the pursuit of education, learning and research at the highest international levels of excellence.

www.cambridge.org
Information on this title: www.cambridge.org/9781009382205
DOI: 10.1017/9781009382229

First published 2024

Printed in the United Kingdom by TJ Books Limited, Padstow Cornwall

A catalogue record for this publication is available from the British Library.

Library of Congress Cataloging-in-Publication Data
Names: Gregory, Robin (Robin Scott), 1950- author. | Moore, Brooke (College teacher), author.
Title: Sorting it out : supporting teenage decision making / Robin Gregory, University of British Columbia, Vancouver, Brooke Moore, District Principal, Delta, BC, Canada.
Description: Cambridge, United Kingdom ; New York, NY : Cambridge University Press, 2024. | Includes bibliographical references and index.
Identifiers: LCCN 2023027728 | ISBN 9781009382205 (paperback) | ISBN 9781009382229 (ebook)
Subjects: LCSH: Decision making in adolescence.
Classification: LCC BF724.3.D47 G74 2024 | DDC 155.5/13–dc23/eng/20230728
LC record available at https://lccn.loc.gov/2023027728

ISBN 978-1-009-38220-5 Paperback

A book for people who live or work with kids

Contents

Territory Acknowledgment

We live and teach on the unceded territories of Indigenous Peoples who have been stewards of this land for millennia, Robin on the lands of the Shíshálh Nation, Brooke on the lands of the Musqueam and the Tsawwassen First Nation. We acknowledge our deepening awareness that Indigenous Peoples' ways of being and knowing often emphasize many qualities also found in the thinking characterized by the Decision-Maker Moves – listening carefully, encouraging dialogue, embracing multiple values, taking a long-run perspective, and constructing resilient options. We offer our respect to First Peoples who have long-standing languages and practices for making sense of the world and coming to decisions within and as community.

If you are curious about the land on which you live, work, and play, consider learning more; https://native-land.ca can be a helpful place to start.

About This Book

While working on this book, Brooke stopped in at her good friend Ellen's house for coffee. Ellen's fifteen-year-old was just heading out the door as Brooke took off her jacket.

"Be smart out there!" Ellen yelled after her daughter.

Normally, Brooke would have made a wry comment about what Ellen was like at that age, but she had this book on her mind so instead she asked Ellen what she meant by smart.

"Oh you know, it's just so scary out there. Who knows what she'll get into. I don't want her to make a bad choice that will ruin her life."

As a former high school teacher and now a parent, Brooke knew exactly what type of trouble Ellen meant. And yet, the interaction made her wonder – what did Ellen mean by "be smart" and "don't … make a bad choice"? Did she mean be smart *as in "make the choices I want you to make" or* be smart *as in "make the choices you can be proud of as you figure out who you are becoming." Obviously, we all want our kids to be safe but we also want them to think for themselves – especially when it really counts and as they grow up and begin making consequential choices all on their own.*

You want kids to make good decisions, but you cannot program them with answers to all the situations they will encounter. Instead, you need them to be able to think things through on their own, in a reliable and intelligent way. You want to send them into the world confident enough to ask the right questions and anticipate consequences they are likely to encounter. Even – or especially – when their final choices are not the same as yours.

Decisions provide opportunities. Younger children are offered choices that start with small things, like what shirt they want to wear or what book they want to read. As they grow up these choices shift to what style of clothes to wear and who to hang with as friends, moving on to decisions dealing with political views, sharing of on-line information, how they express their gender and sexuality, drugs and alcohol, employment and job training. As older teen-agers they will be out in the world, often acting independently from the adults in their lives, making decisions that cumulatively shape *their* lives.

Our focus is on ways that you – an important adult in the life of one or more teenagers – can support youth aged ten to twenty (or thereabouts) as they face the nonstop flow of decisions in their lives. With a little decision science tucked in your back pocket, your support and encouragement can be part of a conversation that helps ensure the youth you care about are ready to face the many choices that lie ahead of them. In some cases, a few minutes of fo-cused attention from a trusted adult can make a real difference in the way a kid looks at a decision, perhaps changing what seemed like an insurmountable problem to a decision opportunity with several possible solutions. Maybe you also want to become a more confident decision maker yourself – that's a big plus from our standpoint, because so few of us adults received training in making good decisions. (Can you remember taking a course on making good decisions at your middle or high school? No, we can't either.)

These pages will introduce you to six *Decision-Maker Moves*. Each move highlights practical skills for making better choices. Decision makers of any age can develop and apply these skills to the small decisions they make each day and the larger decisions that come once a month, once a year, or once in a lifetime.

The decision-making approach we describe is grounded in dec-ades of science generated from all around the world (you didn't know that decision making is a science? Don't worry! Neither did

Brooke, before she met Robin). The six Decision-Maker Moves have been tested in a wide range of settings from dinner tables to classrooms, boardrooms, and beyond. The approach requires (and helps to develop) self-knowledge – knowing what matters to you – and awareness of what matters to others. As teachers for many years, both in K-12 and in universities, we consider these to be essential skills for a diverse and fast-changing world – one that for many young people too often feels confusing and overwhelming.

Simply put, our goal is for youth to partner with the adult mentors in their life – parents, teachers, coaches, grandparents, family friends, aunts and uncles – and change their go-to behaviours, not simply memorize (and rarely apply) yet another protocol. Why? Because when a youth is standing outside school after classes end for the day or hanging out at the park or mall, whether they function as a good decision maker will depend on their quick response, their second-nature behaviours and reactions – the thoughts and feelings they have learned to bring to every decision, not just the ones somehow marked as "special." And who knows: what looks like a routine, minor choice could turn out to be critical, perhaps because of consequences not thought about at the time.

The choices that are clearly complex and significant might require a teenager to work carefully through all six of the Decision-Maker Moves. However, even in many immediate decision situations, a youth's well-practised decision-making skills can create new habits and lead to new understandings that make a big difference. Feedback from students, teachers, parents, and other kids and adults we've worked with – in schools and government offices, urban centres and rural Indigenous communities, across a broad spectrum of ages, locations, and cultural backgrounds, and in our own homes – demonstrates the power and flexibility of using an improved decision-making process, one that cuts through confusion and helps sort out what's important to consider. Day by day, step by step, making better choices can lead to a more desired quality of life – one more expressive of the unique personality, talents, and experience of each young decision maker.

In each chapter, you will read about kids who have made choices, both good and bad, and the adults who have supported them in the process. You will learn a few simple and empowering techniques for clarifying what a young person values and for thinking creatively about options – stretching beyond the obvious to explore new possibilities. We changed the names of the people in the stories, with four exceptions: (a) Abhay, whom you'll meet later when we share why he made the decision to start a youth organization, (b) Malala, who won a Nobel Peace Prize, (c) Kim, a school principal, and (d) Joanne Calder, a teacher. But more on them later.

At the end of each chapter, we provide a quick summary of the main ideas in a section titled *For Your Back Pocket* – these summary points highlight the most important bits from each chapter. We hope the youth in your life tuck these key takeaways in their back pocket, so to speak, so they will have them ready-to-go when needed. Following these summary points you'll find a checklist of the relevant *Decision Traps* – ways the human brain and heart can prompt us to make poor decisions – and a few bonus ideas that can be used to *Practise* the content of each chapter. Each chapter closes with a brief *Go Deeper* section that lists books, novels, comics, YouTube clips, or movies to turn to if you find the ideas in that chapter deeply interesting and desire to learn more.

Making good choices is a learnable skill – let's learn to do it well.

By the end of this book, our hope is that you and the kids you support will know how to use the Decision-Maker Moves on a wide variety of choices, ranging from the minor decisions made every day to the staggering, once-in-a-lifetime choices that create stress, confusion, and frustration for many of us. We would be ecstatic to hear that the decision-making approaches outlined in this book have helped, in ways small and large, to cut through confusion and replace the stress of solving decision *problems* with the excitement of creating decision *opportunities.*

Our goal is to encourage kids and adults to become familiar with an easy-to-grasp and flexible process that will lead to making better choices. By bundling these ideas as Decision-Maker Moves, and by highlighting some of the ways people frequently go off track when making decisions, we hope to make it easy for youth to improve their decision-making skills and recognize the power of their own decision-making opportunities. And we hope to encourage teenagers to recognize they have the power to make a choice and not just go along with old habits or new friends. As the great basketball player Michael Jordan once said (echoing the words of hockey player Wayne Gretsky): "You miss a hundred percent of the shots you don't take" (quoted in the *Grand Valley Lanthorn*, November 21, 2019).

That's our bottom line: influence and agency can be derived from the choices youth make. Supporting the young people you care about as they sort out their choices – listening to them, talking with them, sharing stories from your own youth or your workplace – will enhance their lives. What's our stake in this? We don't care about whether you see the world in the same way we do. We don't care about your political views or how you feel about social mobility or whether you think government has too much or too little influence on our lives. However, as educators and parents, we *do* care deeply about supporting and encouraging teenagers as they discover their own voice and use this agency to express themselves more fully in their world now and in the one they are creating.

Introduction to the Decision-Maker Moves: The Big Picture

Decisions are doors that provide people of all ages with opportunities to express who they are and to learn about who they want to become. Sometimes the young people in your life may choose the wrong door and, while that can make for a good learning experience, you probably want to help them make good decisions and avoid the bad ones. You did, after all, decide to open up this book. While we cannot program kids with the answers they need to live healthy and fulfilling lives, we *can* support kids in learning and using a common-sense approach to understanding and organizing their feelings and thoughts as they make their own decisions.

The Role of the Decision Mentor

Helping a young person make good choices, on their own or in collaboration with others, requires behaviours that naturally incorporate the decision maker's interests yet leave room for inquiry, scepticism, and creativity. Being an effective **decision mentor** means supporting youth in making choices consistent with the decision-making context and *their own interests,* circumstances, capabilities, and talents. The implication for adults is that it's helpful to get your own decision-maker moves in order. After all, the best way for a decision mentor to show kids how to make better decisions is to make conscious, well-considered choices yourself.

You can help the kids in your life expand their options and make choices in line with who they are and what they want – choices that will inform and enrich their lives.

What Does a Decision Mentor Do?

- listens to and is curious about a young person's perspectives and ideas
- helps them recognize there is a choice to make and sort out what's in the picture
- supports the teenager's learning and trusts they will use their voice wisely
- helps a younger person to set realistic goals and expectations
- gives them space and a safe base from which to positively impact their world
- understands that emotions play an important role in thinking, and that both intuition and reflection contribute to making good choices
- models the personal and group dialogue habits that lead to good choices.

The role of the decision mentor is crucial: everyone needs support and encouragement when learning to refine and run with a new skill. Brooke recalls, with the benefit of hindsight, a problem she noticed as a twelve-year-old. While walking home from school, huffing and puffing up a big hill, a car drove past her, sputtering out noxious fumes that she sucked deep into her lungs. Earlier that day her teacher had told the class about the hole in the ozone layer. The fuming car, paired with the lesson, inspired her to start a club. However, the club never went further than the inaugural meeting where she and her friends decided on who would hold each role, from president to treasurer – a model imitated from one of her favourite novels at the time (*The Babysitters Club* series). Meanwhile, on the other side of the country, another twelve-year-old felt inspired about a problem he had just learned about: child labour. Craig Kielburger and his brother went on to create their own club, which evolved into a global organization that has prospered over several decades (and which has since fallen into disrepute due to some questionable choices the founder and his brother made as adults). Now, Brooke isn't saying she could have done the same as that other twelve-year-old – *but* if a decision mentor had helped her frame the ozone problem into a decision opportunity she could do something about, perhaps she could have gone further than one meeting of the (she thinks) cleverly named Oh-zone Club.

How do adults – the pool of decision mentors – typically address decisions? A common approach to making decisions is to make a list of the pros and cons. American statesman Benjamin Franklin wrote about this strategy (in a letter to his friend Joseph Priestley) some 250 years ago:

> ... when uncertainty perplexes us [people should] divide half a sheet of paper by a line into two columns, writing over the one Pro and over the other Con ... When I have thus got them all together in one View, I endeavour to estimate their respective Weights; and where I find two, one on each side, that seem equal, I strike them both out ... I find at length where the Balance lies and I come to a Determination accordingly ... When each is thus considered ... and the whole lies before me, I think I can judge better and am less likely to take a rash step ... (Letter from Benjamin Franklin to Joseph Priestley, September 19, 1772; Franklin 1772/1975, pp. 299–300)

This approach is widely endorsed, partly because the famous Mr. Franklin suggested it and partly because the suggestion to balance gains and losses by thinking through their pros and cons shows great psychological insight. But it can also create problems. As you will see, counting pros and cons ignores many of the most powerful aspects of making good decisions and can lead decision makers astray.

With respect and apologies to Ben, the approach to making decisions we outline in this book goes well beyond simply making a pros and cons list. It is built on, and borrows freely from, well-established practices and writing in psychology, economics, and the decision sciences developed over the past four to five decades. Working together and with others, we've previously described the six Decision-Maker Moves in talks and papers, in books (*Structured Decision Making*, 2012) and as part of a classroom guide for teachers (*The Decision Playbook*, 2019). We also draw on our experiences as parents, our careers in the classroom, and many hours and days spent helping groups of people learn the methods, and in some cases the courage, needed to address tough choices.

Above all, the Decision-Maker Moves reflect a large dose of common sense and a firm belief that making good decisions is a skill, one that can be learned – both essential elements on the road to making better choices. This book focuses on providing techniques and a sequenced approach that will raise the level of decision skills. As with any other skill, success requires practice. This is where your role as decision mentor – a parent or teacher, counsellor or coach, social worker or health practitioner, older family member – is critical, an observation supported by extensive research from psychologists and educators (e.g., Siegel & Bryson, 2012; Carter, 2020). Kids learn best when they have access to a mentor who models the activities and behaviours that underlie good decision making and provides timely insights and suggestions that help a young decision maker improve their skills by paying attention to how they make choices.

Three Spoiler Alerts

1. Decision making is way more than critical thinking. The strengths of a skilled decision maker include compassion, inquiry, scepticism, and open-mindedness to engage in dialogue with people whose perspectives are different. Good decision-making also has as much to do with paying attention to feelings and intuitions as it does with reflective thinking. And it has to do with communication skills, whether the decision maker is acting as an individual or as part of a group.

2. Even if you master all the skills in this book, you'll at times be disappointed by how some of your decisions turn out. There are lots of reasons, including luck and uncertainty, which imply there will also always be surprises – some of which arise because, thankfully, different people hold different values and interpret the world in different ways.

3. Our daily life is full – too full, perhaps – of books and blogs and podcasts which assure you that, if you just follow these simple steps, life will be better. We don't promise you or the youth in your life any such magic – no crystal balls, magicians' wands, or silver bullets. However, the simplicity of the Decision-Maker Moves can help you organize and make sense of the unceasing flow of choices that life

brings. And for youth it can provide a simple and sometimes elegant way to change the anxiety of facing decision *problems* into the joy and richness of exploring decision *opportunities*.

Choices and Decisions

In this book, we use the words *choice* and *decision* interchangeably. However, to a decision scientist:

- **Choice** refers to selecting from among alternatives – for example, whether A or B or C is preferred and, often, to what extent or why.
- **Decision** refers to the larger process of thinking about what is at stake, who is involved, the consequences of different actions, and – eventually – creating the options and asking which is preferred.

How is our approach different from all the others? We recognize that choices will and should vary from person to person and from context to context. Some people rely more on their intuitive side and typically make decisions quickly; others are more reflective and take more time. Options and resources available to some people are unavailable to others. Yet every person has choices to make and their life will in part be shaped by those choices. Making decisions with the Decision-Maker Moves helps a young decision maker reveal or develop their unique personality, talents, and ideas. This is what agency is all about: a young person living their own path with intention and awareness.

The Power to Choose

Kids live in a world of imposed rules: formal and informal, explicit and implied. It may seem like they don't have many real choices, but that's not true. In ways small and large, kids have personal and collective choices about what to do, how to do it, and who to do it with. Cumulatively, the choices they make shape their lives.

Learning to make intentional, conscious choices is an active process of self-questioning. Having access to a decision mentor and to strategies for making good decisions increases the sense of control and ownership kids have over their own lives. The role of the mentor is to help guide young people to be conscious and intentional about how they use their own power – with the understanding that their power is based on, and strongly reflects, the choices they make. In a speech to high-school graduates, writer Julian Aguon said "the only way to successfully make the journey (from adolescence to adulthood) is to learn how to 'get quiet' – that is, to quiet down the noise of other people's opinions and to take instruction instead from one's own heart" (2022, p. 50).

Consider the COVID-19 pandemic that changed the world early in 2020. Everyone was swept into a new decision context, where choices about physical distancing, shared activities, and the future were suddenly and starkly different. No one was sure of the answers. No one really knew what they were battling or which of many proposed strategies would be most effective. Many people were scared, because the virus was new and sometimes deadly. Here is how one father reflects on that time and the decisions his son made.

> "Terrell just about broke me in those early days," recalls Russell. "It was easy at first – when leaving home didn't even seem like an option and we were all terrified of what the news would be saying. But when things started to lighten up, that's when it all kinda blew up on us."
>
> Terrell, it seemed, had had enough of being stuck at home. Almost every night for many months, Terrell snuck out of the house to meet up

with his friends. He didn't see this choice as particularly risky, but when Russell found out what was going on, he didn't know what to say.

"I was like, c'mon man! How are we supposed to see our family – his grandma and my sister and her new baby – if he's out there riskin' our bubble?!"

Terrell just couldn't see how his decisions were impacting others, potentially his extended family or the entire neighbourhood. One night, Russell interrupted his son at the door. The conversation didn't go well and ended with Terrell slamming the door behind him in total defiance of Russell's rules.

This book will provide lots of ideas for how both Russell and Terrell could have looked at this decision in other ways. Perhaps, had they shared the common language of the Decision-Maker Moves and been practising it often, this outcome could have been avoided entirely.

The COVID-19 pandemic also presented elected officials and public health officers with many of the same challenges as those faced by Terrell and Russell. They needed to decide what considerations were most important (avoiding deaths, not overloading hospital facilities, etc.). They needed to know how to hold a dialogue with citizens that would encourage wise decision making, based on everyone listening and learning and adjusting their actions as better information became available. They needed to make many decisions quickly, without access to all the available information. And they needed to know how to identify and address concerns most important to citizens, which often varied across age groups, cultures, and geographic locations.

Rules versus Tools

Adults often offer rules rather than tools or strategies for decision making. In the 1980s, First Lady of the United States Nancy Reagan made a big splash in the media with her slogan "Just Say No" to drugs. The Just Say No campaign was a call to Not Think. It prescribed an outcome but offered no guide for how to make a good choice when faced with the opportunity to try drugs, no distinction between different types of drugs (Beer versus heroin? Offered by a doctor or by a friend?) and no attention to circumstances or social context. The approach took all the power away from a young person and said, "Just obey my simple rule." It didn't work: according to the National Survey on Drug Use and Health, average rates of drug use in the US stayed much the same from the 1980s to the mid-2000s, with more people shifting to opioids and other, potentially deadly pain relievers.

Understanding and paying attention to the many dimensions of an important decision is a fundamental component of making good choices. But it's a hard task, at any age, because it involves keeping in mind the different elements that contribute to why the choice matters and then sorting through them to distinguish what's most important and what actions might be taken. And at a neurological level such multisided choices can be especially difficult for youth because their frontal cortex – where the brain makes sense of the diverse consequences of a pending decision – is still developing.

Consider this mother's response to a difficult choice faced by her daughter.

Fifteen-year-old Sam approached her mom in distress. A friend had just disclosed to Sam that she was obsessed with thoughts of killing herself. Instead of telling Sam what she thought was needed or suggesting that the next steps were beyond her daughter's capabilities, Paige made the choice to keep talking with Sam. Paige knew it was important to combine Sam's powerful emotions about her friend's state of mind with some careful and deliberate thinking. Clearly, time was of the essence, so they moved quickly through a series of Decision-Maker Moves.

    – *First Paige helped Sam frame the problem by asking, "Who should we tell?" Had she framed it another way – "What should we do?"– the next steps would have been quite different. However, Paige knew that they had to inform someone of the situation and quickly. Her question focused Sam on careful thinking in a particular direction.*

- *Then Paige asked, "What's the most important thing here?" She held space for Sam to process her feelings and thoughts, moving Sam out of fear and panic and into a more thoughtful, reflective thinking space. By listening, Paige helped Sam tease out the most important values that she held in this situation – which turned out to be safety and trust. Sam was scared her friend would be angry with her for telling someone the secret. And Paige and Sam both realized that everyone would need to live with and (hopefully) feel okay about their actions over the long term.*

- *Sam and Paige then came up with options: tell the school counsellor, talk with the girl's parents, or talk with her mom. They talked through what was most likely to happen if these options were selected, what would go well, and what might go awry.*

- *Both agreed the best choice was to talk with the girl's mom, and that the meeting should be in person and right away. Sam recognized why safety was more important than keeping the secret and she felt a little more confident about how things were unfolding.*

- *The next step was clear: take action, call the mother to set up a time to talk, and get together immediately.*

The Decision-Maker Moves enabled Paige and Sam to wade through complex emotions while thinking their way carefully towards action. All the while, Paige was able to preserve – and perhaps deepen – her relationship with her daughter. Had she responded by imposing an answer, Sam wouldn't have felt any agency or ownership over the solution – an outcome that could have damaged their relationship and given Sam pause before confiding in her mom the next time she needed support.

Paige's guidance gave Sam the opportunity to connect her emotions (what feels right) with her logic (what makes sense). Thinking through what matters and comparing different options – rather than just going with what feels right at first – gives an individual ownership over their choice. Because of this, a decision becomes a reflection of who the person is. Rather than just "solving a problem," it becomes an opportunity to assert their personal sense of agency and to make a difference, to their own lives and potentially to the lives of others.

One clear lesson from these two examples is that simply imposing a set of rules, without providing a convincing set of reasons, usually doesn't work well. Most people – and certainly most teenagers – don't like being told what matters to them, what to do, or what is possible. Imposing rules also encourages a mindset that says: I know your rule but this situation is different, so I don't have to pay attention to it. And overarching rules can foster dissent: everything becomes an exception, a context where the rules don't have to be followed.

The Decision-Maker Moves

The Decision-Maker Moves clear the way for a person of any age to make better choices. They can help you gain more clarity about your own values, the concerns of others, and the consequences of different actions. Just as learning skills for driving a bicycle or car can help avoid accidents, having access to the Decision-Maker Moves can help avoid many of the traps of poor decision making. With the benefit of some advance planning, the moves apply equally to quick, time-sensitive decisions made in seconds as well as to slower, more relaxed decisions discussed over days or weeks. The key is to recognize that a choice exists and that different futures can unfold depending on what one chooses and how that choice is made.

Here are brief descriptions of each Decision-Maker Move – with more background, examples, and stories to come in the following chapters.

1. **Frame the decision.** Do your best – knowing you're at the beginning of a decision-making process – to understand the context and scope of the decision. It's like you are making a quick sketch of the decision before jumping in, as a way to alert yourself and others about the important issues, key players, and any obvious trouble spots that might lie ahead. For instance, your kid, Lara, may waver between going to a party or not going. You could help her reframe the choice to open up more possibilities: *How can I best relax and connect with my friends this weekend?*

2. **Clarify what matters.** Get to the heart of what matters to the person (or people) making the decision. Let's say Lara finds parties stressful. Since the decision is now about how she can best relax and connect with friends, she can consider what matters most in the context of relaxing and connecting with friends. For example, she might value doing something outside because that is when she is most relaxed. Or she might prefer hanging only with her best friends rather than a lot of acquaintances. Bringing values into the decision frame will invite new insights and options.

3. **Generate options.** Coming up with decision alternatives involves creative and reflective thinking. No longer confined to the binary choice (whether to party or not to party), Lara's options might now include (1) go to party, (2) go bike riding with friends, (3) ride bikes first and then go to party, (4) go camping with friends, or (5) invite two or three of her best friends over instead of going to the party.

4. **Explore consequences.** This Move is about predicting the outcomes of different actions and relating them back to what Lara wants in this context. Some consequences are relatively easy to predict – like checking the forecast to see if rain is expected that night. Other consequences are more problematic: will camping meet her desire to

relax and connect with friends, or will it end up being tons of work and bring on too many arguments? This is where uncertainty can enter – it's impossible to know in advance if they will have arguments while camping or not. Lara could consider past camping experiences and times spent with her friends, but much will remain unknown.

5. **Weigh trade-offs, prioritize, and choose.** Because different actions result in different consequences, getting more of one thing we care about often means we end up with less of something else we also care about. For example, Lara might find that being at a campsite with a few close friends rather than the party with many acquaintances better matches her values, so it's a trade-off she is willing to make. However, if she gets super anxious at the idea of missing out, then perhaps she will stay with the choice of the party. Whatever Lara decides, her decision should reflect her values and make sense in terms of who she is and what matters most to her.

6. **Stay curious and learn.** Making a choice is great, but there is a lot for a teenager to learn from staying connected to the thinking behind the choice and keeping in tune with how it turns out. Staying curious and flexible about the outcomes of our decisions helps us to become better prepared for other similar decisions in the future. It might be better to do something a little different the next time – and staying flexible and making adjustments are characteristics of a good decision maker. Feeling that you have to get everything right the first time and refusing to change your mind is more often a sign of stubbornness than a mark of competent decision making.

The Decision-Maker Moves are based in ideals of listening, awareness, learning, diversity, and a blend of heart and head ways of knowing. Each of the Moves, done well, can help youth enjoy a better decision process and an improved outcome. In many situations all that's needed is to pay attention to one or two of the Decision-Maker Moves: frame the problem in a different way, or search for consequences that might not be immediately obvious.

Decision-Maker Moves

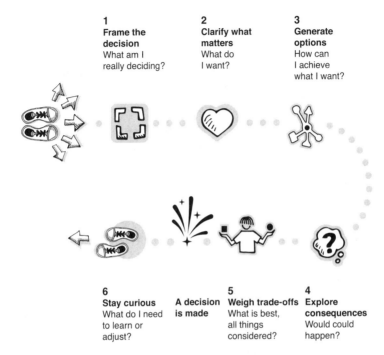

1
Frame the decision
What am I really deciding?

2
Clarify what matters
What do I want?

3
Generate options
How can I achieve what I want?

6
Stay curious
What do I need to learn or adjust?

A decision is made

5
Weigh trade-offs
What is best, all things considered?

4
Explore consequences
Would could happen?

When the decision is more complex or the outcomes more significant, it may be necessary and well worth the extra effort to work through all the Moves.

Decision-Maker Move thinking has been in widespread use for decades and has helped individuals, groups, governments, and industry make better choices and reduce the occurrence of minor and major disasters. And yet knowledge of how to do this sort of thinking is not as common or widespread as it should be, for adults or for kids. Until now. As a decision mentor, you will be in the position to gift this thinking to the kids in your care. And it's a powerful gift – a map they can use to navigate their lives.

Having a Voice and a Choice

Author James Rebanks writes that his early school experiences made him think that "modern life is rubbish for so many people. How few choices it gives them. How it lays out in front of them a future that bores most of them ... How little most people are believed in" (2015, p. 103). Rebanks connects having a voice with making real and significant choices – thereby avoiding becoming bored or, in his evocative words, living a life that's rubbish.

Daniel Pink, who wrote a book about boosting internal motivation with autonomy, purpose, and mastery (*Drive*, 2009), also reminds us that the more choice we have in a matter, the more internally motivated we will be. Teachers know all about this dynamic between motivation and autonomy: "voice and choice" has become a curriculum rallying cry in many countries.

So how can you go beyond offering kids small choices like what book to select during silent reading, what foods to eat on their birthday, or what topic to choose for a science project? These small choices are good starting places for the bigger decisions they will face when you aren't there to help them. The more practice you offer in making decisions that have an impact on their lives, the more prepared the kids in your life will be when they face a choice you neither designed nor anticipated for them.

- **If you are a parent**, to what extent do you decide what's best on behalf of your kids and to what extent does your child also have a say? What issues or topics are open to some form of shared decision making? What does having a voice look like? Can they decide their own hair style? Do your kids have a say in consequential family decisions? At what age does some sharing of power and acknowledgment of input to choices begin?
- **If you are a teacher**, how much and when do you involve your students in designing their learning? Do you set their projects or are

your students given choices about their assignments? Do you assign a grade or co-construct it? How open are you to students' suggestions for new ways to support their learning?

- **If you are a youth counsellor, sports coach, or after-school programmer**, are kids setting priorities and offering program input? Some programs severely constrain where students have a voice in decisions, whereas other programs open up and explore the concept of voice and choice – even including learners in decisions about program goals and budgets.

- **If you are a health professional,** how much do you engage the youth you work with in identifying and naming what is important to them? Do you set out and enforce goals and methods or do you help them use their own creativity and experience to partner with you in considering a variety of choices and pathways?

Everyone has a deeply rooted desire to have a say in things that matter to them. As a decision mentor your goal is to support others in learning how to make the best decisions they can. Of course, opportunities to exercise the Decision-Maker Moves will vary among people. Some youth have ample resources and freedom to experience the joys of agency and the excitement of creating new actions and alternatives. But many do not: poverty and a wide range of social inequities can limit realistic options. The most obvious constraint for decision mentors, perhaps, is time: if you are a single parent with a full-time job, you may have less time to sit down and carefully work through a tough choice with your kids. Our hope is that educators also play a role in this aspect of kids' development, and that other trusted adults can step in and help youth gain perspective on a decision. After all, it takes a village.

Being a competent decision maker opens doors and it helps to level the playing field. For all of us who work or live with kids, ensuring they are taught good decision-making skills is equity work. This powerful skill set helps them engage in the world with an increasing sense of confidence and agency from wherever their story starts.

How Kids Make Choices

Youth face a myriad of choices every day. Many decisions are familiar and relatively easy to make, with only minor implications. Other choices are more significant and can place the decision maker in uncomfortable or dangerous situations. Choices can create opportunities, but they can also create anxiety and confusion. Here are some areas where decisions could have big implications for kids' futures:

- Sharing personal information online
- Experimenting with drugs
- Coming out about their sexuality
- Deciding whether to take a self-defence class
- Sharing a compromising photo online
- Dealing with bad behaviour from a boss or supervisor
- Taking performance-enhancing drugs
- Accepting or turning down a job offer
- Staying with, or quitting, a school sports team
- Deciding whether (and where and in what) to pursue post-secondary education
- Choosing who to be in a relationship with or whether to end a relationship
- Selecting which school clubs to join
- Deciding which extracurricular activities to participate in
- Deciding how much alcohol (if any) to drink at a party
- Going to an unsupervised party
- Wearing traditional clothing or religious symbols
- Telling an adult about an unsafe activity either witnessed or participated in

And these are just individual circumstances. There are also societal decisions young people make that can have significant consequences for themselves or their families and communities. Here are a few:

- Deciding whether to join a local political party or group
- Deciding whether and how to protest against practices they find upsetting
- Choosing whether to follow a teacher or health expert's advice
- Standing up at school for a friend or a marginalized individual
- Being curious about someone's perspective that is very different from their own
- Figuring out whether and where to volunteer after school
- Choosing to stay or move away from home after high school
- Coming up with a plan to reduce their family's environmental footprint

Making these societal decisions in a healthy, self-determining way requires a younger person to understand their own feelings and reasons along with the feelings and reasons of others who may hold slightly or radically different beliefs. The Decision-Maker Moves, with their emphasis on clarifying what matters and exploring different choice options, prompt young decision makers to navigate these rough waters while working cooperatively with others.

What processes do kids typically use to deal with decisions when they have the freedom to choose? Here is what classroom teachers and students tell us:

- If the decision is individual, they often will go with their instincts, with how they feel.
- If feeling conflicted, they may talk with friends or tally up a pros and cons list covering several options, sometimes in writing but usually in their head.
- If the decision involves unknown consequences, they may check with friends or do an internet search.
- If the decision is collaborative, they'll briefly discuss and then vote, going with whatever option wins a majority or the opinion of the individual with the most influence.

Although these different strategies are familiar, they do not *reliably* end in good decisions. Going with their instincts will ignore potentially useful information that can only be assessed through a more thoughtful, patient approach. Likewise, pros and cons lists oversimplify matters because they don't allow for context or that some items on the list matter more than others. And following the suggestions of the loudest voice in a crowd offers others more influence than they probably deserve.

How Decision Making Changes as People Age

Understanding developmental impacts on decision making is an active area of research, with new insights coming all the time. At this point, several things are clear. Younger brains tend to have shorter attention spans, so focusing for long periods can be more difficult. This is because the prefrontal cortex is still developing, as is the ability to understand and respond to others' feelings (a common definition of empathy). And future planning can be difficult: younger brains place a relatively higher value on the benefits of short-term returns (having fun, hanging out with friends) and less on the risks associated with longer-term consequences (getting in trouble, losing privileges). This dynamic means the risk–reward balance is tilted in favour of short-term gains, which may frustrate decision mentors. Research also shows that teenagers who have access to adults talking through the tough choices benefit from this broadened perspective and, as a result, tend to exhibit lower overall levels of risk-taking behaviour (Qu et al., 2015).

Two Modes of Thinking

Fortunately, the social sciences have much to say about making good choices. A major recent insight from decades of observation and research is that humans make decisions, big and small, using two modes of thinking. One is fast (sometimes automatic) and linked closely to emotions and intuition; it's referred to as System 1. Another is slower and involves more reflection and effort; it's referred to as System 2.

The first insights into these two systems of thinking came from brain researchers, whose work in the 1990s provided new insights into the capabilities of the adolescent brain. It has been shown that the ability to do more reflective and analytic thinking increases with age because the brain changes over time, with the prefrontal cortex still developing through the adolescent years. Yet even though adults can access System 2 thinking more easily, listening to System 2 takes effort. Neuroscience research shows that our brains like to conserve energy and using the more effortful System 2 requires more energy than System 1. So to some extent, we are biologically wired to use the automatic and fast-acting System 1 even when more reliance on System 2 would serve us better. This preference for fast thinking can be a barrier to good decision making. Everyone needs to learn when it's worthwhile to question our first instincts in the light of overlooked values, neglected decision participants, or omitted consequences.

Psychologists Daniel Kahneman, Amos Tversky, and Paul Slovic have led behavioural research into these two modes of thinking. The results clearly show that fast and slow thinking are usually both at play and, often, intertwined. When you meet someone new, for example, your intuitive System 1 kicks in right away and quickly sends you signals based on first impressions, which are often rooted in earlier experiences. Over time, your more reflective and analytic thinking may adjust this first impression (for better or worse). On the other hand, when you're learning a new skill you will generally rely on slow thinking at the start. Remember learning to ride a bike or drive a car? It starts out as a painful series of conscious manoeuvres and then, quite quickly, becomes second nature. After that, your automatic thinking usually guides you but only until your car's warning system flashes red lights or your bike gets a flat tire. Then you need to very quickly become effortful and engage your slower thinking system to deal effectively with the situation.

Fast and Slow Thinking

System 1 (*FAST thinking*)

System 2 (*SLOW* thinking)

- operates automatically, with little or no effort
- makes simple associations from emotional reactions
- highlights recent, sensational experiences
- emphasizes immediate or short-term solutions
- doesn't handle numbers or abstract concepts

- takes reflection and effort
- recognizes relationships among outcomes
- balances values and addresses trade-offs
- focuses on long-term solutions
- understands math, proportions, and numbers

Concepts like fast and slow thinking and other findings from the decision sciences are filtering into classrooms and curricula. Yet the still-forming adolescent brain presents real challenges for any approach intended to help youth make better decisions. Younger people may have trouble managing and regulating their emotions, and they may not yet have a firm grip on concepts such as cause and effect. Peer pressures – especially strong in the teenage years – can encourage a "go along with the group" reflex and make it difficult to activate more thoughtful, reflective thinking. And the adolescent brain is likely to give more weight to short-term consequences because the longer-run outcomes of today's decisions are, well, a long way off.

Anticipating the Pull and Power of System 1 Emotional Reactions

Although it's true that research into the distinctions between our emotions-driven, automatic System 1 and slower, more reflective System 2 is quite recent, knowledge of the phenomenon has been around for thousands of years. A classic story from ancient Greece, told by poet Homer in the *Odyssey* (and read by generations in the intervening 2,800 years), follows the hero Odysseus in his journey home after fighting the Trojan War for ten long years. Aided by advance advice from the sorceress Circe, Odysseus plugs the ears of his crew with wax and ties himself securely to the mast of his ship, so he could enjoy the lovely Sirens' song while voyaging home but not fall prey to their temptations (and thereby crash his ship on the rocks and drown). In the same way that information provided by Circe helped Odysseus use proactive thinking and escape the deadly peril of the Sirens, the task of the decision mentor is to help the youth they know access information about the risks and dangers associated with temptations that range from misuse of drugs to bullying to unwelcomed sexual behaviours. We can't shield the kids in our lives from exposure to emotionally appealing yet dangerous interactions, but we can prepare youth to recognize these situations, make good decisions, and stay safe by anticipating what might occur and embracing a broader perspective.

Adolescence is also characterized by *In* groups and *Out* groups. The desire to belong is understandably strong when young people are working out who they are in a world that may feel confusing or scary. It's natural to identify with the views of a particular group. However, good decision making depends on knowing what matters to oneself, which may or may not align with what matters to others. Simply being aware of the distinction between faster and slower modes of thinking can provide a nudge that helps young decision makers plan ahead or take a few extra seconds to clarify their own values and concerns before making a choice.

There is no doubt that this mix of contextual, neurological, and psychological factors makes for a complicated and, at times, tough journey. Neither intelligence nor creativity will guarantee safe passage to a fulfilling adult life. Along the way there will be ample opportunities to favour short-term gains over long-term goals, and there will be people who seek to manipulate or misguide younger people. For example, many product manufacturers recognize the massive buying power of individuals aged 12–20 and maintain large numbers of staff dedicated to encouraging purchases (after little or no reflection) on the part of teenagers. Knowing even a little about good decision making and the fast versus slow thinking distinction can reduce the vulnerability of younger people to such outside influences.

As a skilled decision mentor, you can offer a safe space for kids to pause and reflect and gain confidence in the wisdom of their own perspectives. Through dialogue and by example, you can help them clarify what really matters, see the bigger picture and talk openly with their peers and others, and (as much as possible) anticipate future consequences of their current actions. Self-knowledge is fundamental to good decision making: you can't go for more of what you want unless you know what it is you are wanting.

Decision Traps

The world can be fast paced, with many things happening at once. Too many inputs, too much noise, misinformation, competing interests – it can feel overwhelming. When we try to make sense of what we want and what information is relevant, humans of all ages are influenced by a range of mental shortcuts, ways in which our natural decision-making tendencies may lead us astray.

The identification and detailed study of ***decision traps*** – also known as judgmental biases or mental heuristics – is recent. For much of the twentieth century, it was widely thought that people were basically rational and would use available information as part of a considered, thoughtful decision-making process. Then in the early 1970s, cognitive psychologists began exploring the disconnects between the assumptions about human behaviour and what people actually do when making decisions in the real world. It turns out that humans often

- are not rational actors
- keep doing something even after they realize it's not working
- are overly influenced by highly evocative events

- are not swayed by facts that contradict their point of view
- are overly confident about their own abilities and understanding

Decision traps are a universal decision-making hazard for people of any age, from any country and culture, and with any level of training (from novice to expert). Three of the most common decision traps are *anchoring*, *numbing*, and *availability* – we introduce these now and bring in more traps as part of later chapters. As with the sailor Odysseus, becoming familiar with each of these traps in advance makes it easier to recognize when you or others are falling into one and often (but not always) avoid the trap and make a good decision.

Anchoring

Anchoring is the tendency to settle on a single idea and stick with it even if subsequent information calls for a rethink. First impressions can be useful – like kicking the tires on a used vehicle to check on its condition or guessing at someone's interests by looking around the first time you're invited to their house. But it's also important to pause and leave space to adjust this initial view when new information comes along. For example, a student might do poorly on a math test and decide, once and for all, that they're not very good at math even if they do better on later exams. Or a new kid might be judged as "a little weird" by classmates on their first day of school and not be given a fair chance as the year goes on. Moments like these can affect how we see the world, or how other people view us, for a very long time unless we are open to new learning.

Anchoring Occurs Even When It's Clearly Wrong-Headed

Even though some of the classic studies of anchoring were conducted by Kahneman and Tversky nearly fifty years ago (Kahneman & Tversky, 1984), the bias continues to play a role in many decisions that youth (and, sadly, their decision mentors) make. In one of the early studies subjects were asked several questions designed to test their knowledge of facts about which they were likely to be uncertain, such as the proportion of African nations that were members of the United Nations (think for a minute: what would your answer be?). The researchers discovered that subjects were hungry for cues that would help guide how they should answer, even if the cues had nothing at all to do with the question at hand. As one example, responses were influenced by spinning a wheel of fortune (similar to a roulette wheel) in front of subjects to generate what was clearly a random number. When a big number showed up on the wheel the average estimates of African nations in the UN increased significantly, whereas when a small number showed up the estimates declined.

Numbing

Another common trap is to feel numbed by stories that describe events using big numbers (e.g., thousands of people affected by a flood, or billions of dollars spent on a vaccine). At such times the mind seems to just shut down: it's easier not to pay attention and simply move on. Psychologist Paul Slovic and others call this phenomenon *psychic numbing*. People tend to feel more distress and express more compassion when considering a single person in need – especially when given a face and a name – than when considering the needs of four people, or eight, or tens of thousands (Slovic et al., 2017). Once the numbers spike, numbing sets in and compassion collapses. It's a great example of the triumph of System 1's automatic response over System 2's slower thinking: fast thinking pays a lot of attention to emotions but doesn't pay any attention to numbers.

American writer Annie Dillard has used the term "compassion fatigue" to describe how our minds go to sleep in the face of tragedies involving large numbers of people (Dillard, 1999). How can the suffering of one person be more upsetting and more motivating than the suffering of thousands? Because as soon as individuals become statistics it's far too easy to lose touch with them. Thankfully, creating more concrete images can help reignite compassion. For example, in 2015 the photograph of a young Syrian boy named Alan Kurdi lying dead on a beach was viewed by more than 20 million people on social media and resulted in a large boost in donations to help refugees. Why? Everyone could recognize a little boy they know and love in that desperate image. Reframing information can also help to cut through compassion fatigue: a civil war that has displaced 400,000 people over the last fifty days can be reframed as displacing one person every eleven seconds – still a statistic, but now more meaningful because it is easier to connect with.

Compassionate Thinking

Compassion refers to a concern for others who are suffering or in distress. Compassionate thinking, which combines System 1 fast feelings and System 2 slow reflection, underlies the work of many charities as well as local and international efforts – ranging from soup kitchens to music festivals – that seek to provide relief for those whose lives are challenged by poverty or upended by war, floods, fires, or drought. Many writers, musicians, and media stars have noted a disturbing trend in decisions made by citizens toward a more narrow and individual focus. Yet it's also true that many teenagers – perhaps encouraged by today's quick access to media reports and photographs of events taking place in other countries – are taking a lead role in seeking to broaden society's perspectives and shift resources (food, money, aid) from those who have more to others – whether on the other side of town or the other side of the globe – who have less or are at risk, remembering that compassionate decisions can focus on helping people, plants, or animals. As a decision mentor you can help youth you support think creatively about options and find ways to express compassion in alignment with their values and capacities.

Availability

Availability is when a person is overly influenced by the ideas or images that most quickly come to mind. These easy-to-access images then have a disproportionate influence on the choices made, especially when the information is unusual or sensational and appeals to our emotions. A young adult sees a picture of their favourite celebrity smiling at a restaurant and suddenly they want to go themselves. Or you read a story about a type of car that caught fire on the freeway and you make a mental note to never buy one of those lemons. Advertisers are experts at creating easily available images that hook our attention and control our decision-making process – and firms hire expensive public relations experts to overcome negative images associated with a faulty product.

People will forever deal with choices using a mix of fast emotional responses and slower, more thoughtful reasoning. It's how we're wired. The best way to minimize the influence of these traps is to learn about them. Then it becomes possible to anticipate their pull and take preventive actions.

Is Every Decision a Big Deal?

Kids make hundreds of choices every day. You probably do too. If everyone had to slow down and work through a careful, conscious decision-making process for every choice, we would barely make it out of bed. Thankfully, routine choices are often good enough because, most times, the stakes are low and gut feelings have been educated well by experience and teachings. Yet feelings also deceive, and at times it can be helpful to recognize that the choices at hand require more than habit or intuition. When are these "big deal" decisions most likely to arise for the young people in your life?

- when a situation is novel, so prior experiences don't help
- when the time to choose is limited
- when the consequences of a decision could be significant
- when important information about values or outcomes is highly uncertain
- when outcomes are likely to be irreversible
- when other people are involved in the decision-making process

Time-sensitive decisions are especially important for youth because lots of the choices that come up in an adolescent's life need to be made quickly – sometimes in a few seconds. For example, a teenager is invited to get into a car with a driver who has been drinking. They can't stand there holding the door open and run through the Decision-Maker Moves in their head. Yet the Moves can still go a long way toward informing the decision, providing the decision maker has been prompted to think about this situation in advance and come up with thoughtful principles to guide decisions in those situations where there really isn't time for careful thinking.

It's essential that as a decision mentor you respect the values, concerns, fears, knowledge, and points of view of the young people you're supporting. Whenever you have the privilege of mentoring young decision makers, remember that what you might consider to be a relatively minor decision could matter a lot to them. Where to sit in class, who to work with on a research project, or how much time they spend practising before a big game can all, at the time, feel deeply consequential.

The other "big deal" theme we want to emphasize is that many of the decisions made by kids are not individual choices but part of a shared or group decision-making process. When other people are involved, it can be difficult to make space for healthy conversations across conflicting points of view and for everyone to stay open minded. Instead, it sometimes happens that people become polarized and locked into distinct perspectives through membership in this or that group. Rather than seeking creative, shared solutions through dialogue, people end up in arguments that see each party stubbornly putting forth their own point of view. This conflict carries over to how information is interpreted: what is accurate and helpful to one group can seem like misleading rhetoric to another.

A few years ago one of the authors was given the opportunity to observe (and comment on) the hiring process at a large software company. Not being a computer expert himself, Robin anticipated that the interview process would revolve around tough questions being asked of young people about coding or design issues. Instead, six job candidates were placed in a room and given 90 minutes to solve a problem that had nothing to do with computers or software. Managers from the firm observed how things were going through a one-way mirror. They told Robin the objective of the exercise wasn't to find the smartest or best-trained person in the group but to select the person (or persons) best at working collaboratively when solving a tough problem. Candidates receiving job offers would be respectful of others and have their own ideas – a person who could listen to suggestions and be flexible, then communicate clearly how their choice accounted for the different elements of the assigned problem.

The good news is that a group of people can agree on an action without having to agree about every component of the decision and without having to know about every detail of its outcomes. It's the difference between talking with the intent of convincing others (in the extreme, showing why they are wrong and you are right) and talking from a place of curiosity, with a desire to listen and learn. As you'll discover in later chapters, the Decision-Maker Moves provide simple tools that can assist listening, which is itself a crucial life skill.

The Decision-Maker Moves provide kids with important opportunities to realize agency within their own lives. They will be empowered to make better individual and group decisions and better choices on behalf of their communities, without being as susceptible to their own decision-making traps or overly influenced by the views, ideas, and motivations of others.

31

Good Decisions Sometimes Fail

The Decision-Maker Moves provide a relatively simple, common-sense way to approach a wide range of decisions. The Moves work, but no decision-making process is foolproof. Good outcomes can sometimes follow poor choices, and disappointing outcomes can sometimes follow good choices. You forget to bring a raincoat but it turns out okay because, despite heavy clouds, it doesn't rain until you're home. Or you carefully research what's the best computer to buy but happen to get a defective one that breaks after two weeks. Here are five of the more common reasons why even a good decision might fail.

No Guarantees

Using a good decision-making process increases the likelihood of a good decision outcome, but it does not come with a guarantee. Sometimes a person does everything right – thinks about their values, comes up with a great set of options, collects accurate information on consequences, and considers trade-offs – but the outcome of their decision is not what they planned or hoped for. Maybe an important value was omitted from the decision frame, or maybe a surprising external factor played a role. Or maybe they were just unlucky – a common decision-making mistake is to downplay the role of luck, good or bad, in evaluations of the choices we (and others) make.

> *Sports fans know the feeling: There are twelve seconds left in the big high-school basketball game and the team is trailing by one point. Coach Anderson calls a play designed to get the ball to Karine, the best player on the team and blessed with nerves of steel. Everything works like a charm: Karine gets her open shot with three seconds left, and ... . the ball hits the rim and bounces off. A disappointing outcome, but probably still a good decision by the coach.*

Overconfidence Stifles Curiosity

Being confident is usually an asset, but being overconfident can lead to poor decisions. Overconfidence appears whenever someone so strongly considers their position, or their group's position, to be correct that they find little reason to trust or believe any information suggesting otherwise. Open-mindedness and healthy scepticism are two essential habits for good decision making. To be *open-minded* is to be curious, welcome new perspectives, and pay attention to evidence. To be s*ceptical* means you have the discipline and willingness to scrutinize and question both your own assumptions and those of others. And because being open-minded and sceptical should lead to new learning that complements, rather than undermines, an adolescent's confidence, it's yet another place where a decision mentor can encourage a young person and lead by example.

Abby grew up in a house where the kids were expected to become doctors or lawyers. Her parents, both hard workers, were convinced that their children should get good grades and train for a high-income, white-collar job. As the youngest of five children Abby watched her siblings take on these goals. But Abby felt she was different: she loved to work with her hands and felt most at home in the mechanic shop at her school.

Before entering her final year of high school, Abby talked with her parents. She wanted to enrol in a trades apprenticeship program instead of biology. Her father didn't speak to her for a week. Her mother looked disappointed every time Abby entered a room. Abby felt terrified. She had never caused such a disruption before and she wasn't sure her parents would ever support her. Fast forward, Abby is now an apprenticing heavy-duty mechanic and although her parents aren't thrilled at the path she has chosen for herself they are at least accepting of it.

Uncertainty Is Real

Even the most diligent decision maker won't know everything they'd like to know when making a decision because key pieces of information are either unavailable or uncertain. One of the ways of dealing with uncertainty is to assume that things will go well – which sometimes works out okay and sometimes doesn't. Another way is to pretend there is no uncertainty because all the relevant information is known. These "hide your head in the sand" approaches can lead to unwanted surprises. Uncertainty is a reality in our lives and, while we can't control it, acknowledging it and allowing for a range of outcomes can help us make better decisions. More on this topic later, but for now we note that a good decision-maker response in the face of uncertainty is to be flexible, so as new information becomes available it can be incorporated and, if appropriate, lead to a shift in what is decided.

> *The COVID-19 pandemic of 2020–2022 introduced a burst of uncertainty into the world and led to what is commonly referred to as "supply-chain" issues, where key parts for items were suddenly no longer available. The reasons were varied and often obscure, from production issues to transportation problems and large increases in the cost of fuel or other materials. But the outcomes were obvious: consumers trying to order new bikes and cars were being told it might take up to six months, or even one or two years, before their order would be filled; people all around the world were going to their grocery stores and finding empty shelves, with no idea when the items they were seeking would be back in stock. A common response was surprise and, in some cases (sadly) anger – cashiers in grocery stores and salespeople were too often treated rudely, as if they were somehow responsible for the uncertainty associated with the supply-chain delays. Complicating everything was the uncertainty around how long this situation would last.*

Some Decisions Lack Obvious "Good" Outcomes

What if none of the realistic options have desirable outcomes? This situation is not uncommon: some of the most difficult, and most important, choices faced by teenagers involve using a values-focused approach to choose the least bad option from among a small set of undesirable options. This class of decisions – termed "tragic choices" by one legal scholar – can appear in the context of personal health or job choices as well as social choices involving difficult trade-offs. Yet decisions still need to be made and these will, to a large extent, determine how the experience plays out over time. The role of the decision mentor can be critical in helping a young decision maker slow down and recognize that choices still exist and that they matter.

> Consider the situation faced by Mika, who just made the shift from junior to senior high school. Due to the late timing of her parents' decision to move to a rural town, Mika was left with very few choices for her course scheduling at the nearest high school. She had wanted to take outdoor education or leadership, but those would not fit into her new timetable. Given that an alternate high school was too far away to attend, she had to decide between art and metal work – the only class options still open for new students. This might not seem tragic to you, but she felt otherwise.

In this scenario, a decision mentor could play an important role by offering Mika other ways to think about her limited set of new options. For instance, she might consider which class would be more likely to help her make friends. She might even begin to see some neat possibilities that could arise through giving energy and attention to her (largely neglected) artistic talents. It's a fine line for the decision mentor – too much input could come across as unwelcome optimism – but examples of similar "tragic choices" that worked out well could help, as might some well-timed and delicately worded questions to refocus her attention along the lines of "which teacher seems more friendly?" or "which course has more interesting projects?".

Good Outcomes Aren't All That Matters

Following all the right moves and making a good choice isn't enough to guarantee success if other people need to be convinced the process is sound and the outcome sensible. Good communication skills are important: even the best message, if poorly delivered, won't be well received. Having an open-dialogue matters, and so do the reasons why *this* is chosen over *that*. Knowing and communicating *why* and *how* a decision is made can be as important as the actual choice itself.

So far, our stories have featured youth in the role of decision maker. For this story, we flip the script and, for just a minute, offer you scenarios where the adult is the one making the decision. We do this to make a point and underscore the ways that decisions can break or build trust based on the *process* of the decision – not the decision itself.

When Maevy was young her parents forced her to take swimming lessons. Here is how Maevy describes that decision: "I despised swimming lessons, but I was made to take them because my parents felt it was an important skill. Once I passed all the levels before the lifeguarding levels started, I would be allowed to stop. I hated standing on the side of the pool freezing. I hated the change room. I hated coming outside with wet hair and having it turn to icicles in the cold air. I hated pretending to breathe in someone's face when we did the CPR training. But my parents always made it very clear that I had no say in the matter and that I would thank them later."

Maevy didn't believe that she would thank them later, but she did understand that her parents saw it as a life-skill – something that could keep her safe. She also knew that her parents believed she would get enjoyment and recreation out of being a strong swimmer and, despite Maevy adamantly disagreeing with that position as a child, as an adult Maevy chuckles – turns out she really does love swimming

now, is thankful for her parents' decision, and has enrolled her own
children in swimming lessons despite their frequent protestations.

Clearly Maevy's parents took the long-term view here and Maevy was stuck in the short-term view, mired in the unpleasant sensory aspects of her swimming lesson experiences. It took effort for her parents to enforce their decision – and it made Maevy mad. However, she also accepted the decision, first because she had no choice and second because she trusted that her parents were enforcing it for good reasons – even though she didn't fully understand those reasons at the time.

Obviously, a trusting relationship between you and the young decision makers you support is definitive. Without trust there can be no connection. Sometimes we avoid making tough decisions because we do not want to break others' trust. This strategy, however, promotes false harmony at best and, at worst, can break trust. If the kids in your life can't trust you to hold a line or to make decisions in their interest, who can they trust? So, if you have to make a choice that you know the kids in your life will not like, be sure you can explain your rationale so they can at least trust the why behind your decision. Here are some potential examples of trust-threatening decisions:

- enrolling them in an activity to build certain skills (piano, swimming, language class)
- moving to another town or home
- divorcing your spouse
- enrolling them in a new school
- setting a curfew
- not allowing them to join an activity
- taking them to a doctor

The youth in your life may not endorse your choice at the time, but they can grow to accept it – especially if they trust the process and, sooner or later, get some feedback that helps them to understand where you were coming from.

The Big Picture: For Your Back Pocket

- Making decisions well is not a linear process, but there are clear and proven strategies decision mentors can share with kids to help them navigate through the decision-making jungle of adolescence.

- Facing up to the choices in our lives provides ongoing opportunities for self-expression and discovery. Knowing what matters to oneself is key to good decision making.

- Learning and practising the Decision-Maker Moves can help young people create a life more in line with their values. The role of decision mentors – parents, teachers, coaches, health professionals, older family members – is critical, both for the support they can provide and for the stories of their own decision-making successes and mistakes.

- Everyone makes choices using a mix of faster (automatic) and slower (effortful) thinking. Both ways of thinking are typically part of a good decision-making process.

- Our fast-thinking instincts often provide good guidance, but they can also lead us into making poor decisions unless we're aware of common decision traps and how to reduce their influence on the choices we make.

- There are no guarantees a decision will provide the outcome we hope for. External factors and uncertainty can contribute to unexpected outcomes even for the best-made decisions.

- Until we live in a more equitable society, not everyone will have the same freedom to choose from a range of options when making decisions. Keep in mind the social and cultural contexts and constraints within which young people are making their decisions.

Practice

Think of a young person you live or work with right now. Use the chart shown below to reflect on where you, as the decision mentor, are currently creating decision opportunities for this person and where you are not.

Decisions I get to make (decision mentor)	Decisions _____ (youth) gets to make

Now categorize the decisions in each list. In which types of decisions – or for which areas of life – do you each exert more control?

Next consider asking the young person in your life to fill in their own copy of a chart like this and compare notes.

Decisions I get to make	Decisions my _____ gets to make

Are there some differences? Do the different perspectives – yours as compared to theirs – suggest any shifts that need to be made?

Here's a natural follow-on to this exercise. Look over the two lists once again and choose one thing you will intentionally give the young person more autonomy over – where the stakes are low enough that no one will get hurt or seriously disappointed yet high enough that the outcomes actually matter. Be sure you choose a decision-making space that you won't then take away if they make a decision you don't agree with. For example, if you decide to let your teenage kids make all decisions about hair style, and one or more comes home with an array of streaks and a half-shaved head, you do not get to take away their decision-making powers. Instead, everyone has to live with the results.

Go Deeper

This book is built on, and freely borrows from, many decades of studies and insights completed by other researchers and practitioners in the decision sciences and in education. If it is of interest, you can go deeper into these ideas by checking out the following sources.

– A first source of inspiration is the innovative work by psychologists Daniel Kahneman, Amos Tversky, and Paul Slovic. Kahneman's book *Thinking, Fast and Slow* (Doubleday, 2011) introduces the core elements of good decision making and emphasizes the interplay of faster and slower modes of thinking. We also build on the work of Baruch Fischhoff and Sarah Lichtenstein who for decades have studied how people's perceptions of choices and activities – ranging from smoking cigarettes to owning handguns – are coloured by their feelings and understandings of the trade-offs underlying an acceptable risk (Fischhoff et al., *Acceptable Risk*, Cambridge University Press, 1981; Lichtenstein & Slovic, *The Construction of Preference*, Cambridge University Press, 2006). A summary of early work in this field, often referred to as behavioural decision making, is provided in a widely cited review article by John Payne and colleagues ("Behavioral decision research: A constructive processing perspective," *Annual Review of Psychology*, *43* (1992), 87–131).

- Second, we draw on the insights of a second group of decision-making experts known as decision analysts. In their book Smart Choices (Harvard Business School Press, 1999), John Hammond, Ralph Keeney, and Howard Raiffa introduce examples from their many professional and personal experiences and provide a user-friendly introduction to decision-making skills based on the five-part acronym PrOACT: What is the **Problem**? What are your **Objectives**? What **Alternatives** are possible? What are their **Consequences**? What are the primary **Trade-offs**? Decision analysis approaches are widely used in government and industry to help untangle the various components of a choice and create options that can be supported by different groups.

- A third source is the field of negotiation analysis. Negotiation is basically applied decision making, often with high stakes (and even higher emotions): negotiators need to recognize the nature of the problem, understand the people involved, and, to the best of their abilities, use techniques to help two or more parties move from disagreeing with each other to reaching a solution they can live with. As described by Roger Fisher, William Ury, and Bruce Patton in the long-time best-seller *Getting to Yes* (3rd ed., Penguin Books, 2011), once the parties (and negotiators) are clear about what matters to them, it can be possible to create options that satisfy everyone.

- Several educators also have contributed to the development of critical thinking concepts and to the understanding of decisions educators face. Judy Halbert and Linda Kaser, in particular, encouraged us to write this book. They continue to serve as a model for what is possible in changing outcomes for young people. Their most recent book, *Leading Through Spirals of Inquiry: For Equity and Quality* (Portage and Main Press, 2022), and their network (www.noiie.ca) are helping educators all over the world make decisions focused on improving the experiences of learners.

41

1

Move 1: Frame
the Decision

It's course selection time and Javid, a high school senior, can't decide if he should take the school band option for his one elective, or go with a new course that blends art and technology. He plays the guitar for fun at home and has always wanted to try the sax, but he isn't sure he wants to lug that thing around on his way to and from school. However, the art/tech course is new so he doesn't know anyone who has taken it – and Javid just learned that the teacher is new too, so it's hard to say if she'll be any good. Either way, Javid's parents want him to select something entirely different – a finance course – as his elective because they think it will open more doors later in life than any arts course ever could. Javid is confused. He thought his choice was straightforward but now, with the new information and his parents getting involved, it has become more complicated.

At times like this, when the way forward isn't clear, framing the choice – a quick check into what the decision is all about – can be helpful. And important. Taking control over how we picture the decisions we face is part of transforming decision problems into decision opportunities. The decision frame determines how we bring who we are and what we care about into the decision-making picture.

How we initially frame a choice will inform and influence all the later steps in the decision-making process.

What Is a Decision Frame?

Imagine a photographer, camera in hand, looking out the window of a city building. How will they frame the photo? Maybe they'll focus on the traffic jam one block over, or the unusual hat on the person walking down the other side of the street. Perhaps they'll change lenses and zoom in on the small dandelion growing from a crack in the sidewalk. In the same way a photographer chooses what is visible and what is not, how a decision maker frames a decision determines what is possible and what is not.

Javid could frame his decision in many ways:

- What courses should I take this term?
- How do I get the most out of my high school experience?
- How do I make sure I have the required credits for graduation?
- What doors do I want my coursework to open to me?
- What career do I want?

Each frame leads to a different set of concerns and, ultimately, may lead to different options. That's why it's crucial to help young decision makers frame their choices in ways that make sense to them and that account for the potentially overwhelming variety of factors at play. Without support from a decision mentor a teenager may simply turn away from a decision and go along with ... *whatever* (a favourite word among many teens we know). Or they may end up solving the wrong problem and, as a result, miss out on a great decision opportunity. A supportive mentor can be part of a conversation that helps to sort out what's going on as part of this choice – what's at play, what's possible, and what needs to be decided or acted on now rather than better left until later (by which time additional information may be available).

A key role for the decision mentor is to provide reminders to the young decision maker that framing a choice creates opportunities to see and operate in the world in different ways. With thoughtful guidance and support from a mentor, framing can invite creativity and be an opportunity for the young decision maker to exercise their agency (Yeager, Dahl, & Dweck, 2018). Asking three simple questions can help.

1. Who is in the picture?
2. What is the question?
3. What is the scope?

These powerful questions can clarify the possibilities of any decision.

Who Is in the Picture?

For smaller or more straightforward decisions it's usually fairly obvious who is potentially affected by a choice – oneself, friends, family members, classmates, etc. The implication of leaving someone out of the decision frame is that their views won't influence the choice being made. They could still be affected by the decision but they won't have any influence on the action that's selected.

For larger or more complex decisions, thinking about who is involved becomes a choice in and of itself. Many health decisions change depending on who is involved in the decision frame: a teenagers' decision to follow a friend's lead and try an unknown drug at a party may at the time be framed as a personal decision but the emphasis shifts dramatically if the possible effects on friends, family, and even the health-care system are also taken into account. Another example comes from social decisions where government leaders wrestle with the extent to which future generations will be affected by choices made today and, if so, how much their perspective should count. In Canada, for example, many Indigenous Peoples value what author Bob Joseph calls the Seventh Generation Principle – the principle that all decisions must include consideration of impacts on community members seven generations into the future (Joseph & Joseph, 2019, p. 86). This long-term perspective necessarily impacts how decisions are framed around such questions as the use of fossil fuels or policies protecting endangered species.

What Is the Question?

Consider the importance of clarity in this scenario:

> *Raman wanted to go out with friends and asks her dad if she can. Her dad says yes, assuming the friends in question are the kids Raman has grown up with. Raman grabs her jacket and runs outside, hopping into a car driven by a new friend Raman's dad has never met.*

A common framing mistake is to assume you are being clear when communicating with other people: you know what you're saying so others will too!

Effective communication about choices is always a two-way street. Particularly when decisions are collaborative or outcomes can be significant, it's important to make sure everyone has the same understanding of the questions and the language at the heart of the decision frame. One kid asks another "Want to go camping this weekend?" The first imagines a fun opportunity to be out in the woods; the second perceives an invitation for intimate physical closeness. Your child says "I need help with my history paper." Is this a request for you to get involved or will it result in a phone call with a friend? Is there a need for ongoing support or for specific, one-time assistance?

Are You Clear? Really Clear?

Ralph Keeney is a renowned expert in decision making and a consultant for governments and industries facing tough choices. He tells a great "what's the question" story about a presentation he gave in California to a group of earth scientists. Keeney's talk was designed to encourage clear thinking and foster good decisions about how public officials should deal with the uncertainty associated with earthquakes. He first asked participants to complete a short questionnaire, starting with this question: "Is it true or false that there is a reasonable chance of a moderate to large earthquake in the San Francisco Bay area in the near future?" Everyone answered *True*. Keeney then asked participants to define each of the four key elements that together framed his question: reasonable chance, moderate to large earthquake, San Francisco Bay area, and near future.

As he expected, the participants' responses showed little agreement regarding what the question was asking. For example, one expert defined the San Francisco Bay area as within five miles of downtown while another included a span of over 140 miles in all directions. One said the "near future" meant up to three weeks away; another said it meant the next 100,000 years. You can imagine the sharp differences in the responses of public officials and the messages sent to citizens depending on how they interpreted the question: if a possible earthquake in the "near future" means it could occur in the next three weeks there would be urgent warnings and panicked citizens, whereas if "near future" instead referred to the next 100,000 years residents would probably go about their business as usual.

Despite the huge (and troubling) disparity in these outcomes, the expert participants had happily given answers to what amounted to very different questions because they framed their decisions in dramatically different ways. "What's really surprising about this," Keeney told Robin, "is that the scientists weren't aware of the large variations in how they were defining [i.e., framing] my question" (personal communication).

What Is the Scope?

The third question to consider in framing a decision is its scope. How much should the decision maker zoom in or out on a decision? For instance, when making choices about organizing end-of-year activities, a student council might consider the decision frame and realize there are a lot more options available beyond holding a traditional dance. They could zoom out and ask the open-ended question: How do we want to celebrate the end of the year? This decision process might include consultation with school leadership to come up with a short list of activities, which could then be included in a survey of students. Or they could reframe by zooming in and asking: What style of dance do we want? This decision might include consultation with the student body and local DJs.

A common mistake in framing decisions is to assume too narrow a scope. This omits potentially interesting options, as in the example above. It also omits potentially important consequences. Consider climate change: not long ago climate change was generally referred to as "global warming" due to the effect of CO_2 (and other) emissions on average annual temperatures. A focus on warming led to boosts in sales of air conditioners and thoughts of longer summers. But reframing the scope of the issue – and the language used to describe it – brings in many other factors, like the increased risk of forest fires and loss of animal habitat (to name only two). And maybe all the electricity used to run those air conditioners will make things even worse? These changes in scope – whether the decision frame is larger or smaller – have important implications for policy makers as well as for families and individuals.

This all sounds great: answer three questions to frame a decision and open up new decision-making possibilities. And it's true. However, it's also a human tendency to see the world, and to frame our decision options, in a way that is familiar and perpetuates our current reality. This characteristic is often referred to as the ***status quo trap***, and it makes it easy to miss out on new decision-making opportunities.

Often the best ways to help overcome the power of the status quo is simply to remind ourselves that what is currently going on is only one of many ways of being in the world. Sometimes it helps to ask the decision maker: if things weren't already like they are now, is this what you would choose? If not, what changes can realistically be made to help the decision maker get to a new place, one they might well prefer?

Decision framing is an exercise in strategy and creativity. If decision makers start with the right decision frame – one that makes sense to them – the final outcomes will prove far more meaningful.

Framing Matters

Let's go back to Javid and his decision about what elective to take. How he frames his decision will impact the action he takes. Javid needs to frame his course selection decision realistically regarding

- his ability to implement the decision
- the decisions he needs to make now versus those he can make later
- any direct constraints on his choices

Part of what turns a decision *problem* into a decision *opportunity* is recognizing the increased flexibility that goes along with how the decision is framed. And because it takes place early in the decision-making process, framing or *reframing* a problem often allows the decision maker to insert their own preferences and exercise agency. In some cases, the choice of a frame will go a long way toward resolving whatever issue or concern has prompted the need for a decision in the first place.

When a young person comes to you with a decision they are struggling to make, they probably already have landed on a decision frame – but in most cases they will have done so unconsciously. So right at the start of your conversation it's worth checking to see if the decision they are wrestling with is actually the decision they want to be making. Perhaps the goal of the decision is unrealistic. Or perhaps you get a feeling that someone else has framed the decision for them. Thoughtfully considering (and sometimes altering) the decision frame helps a young decision maker gain more ownership over their choice and build their sense of agency. Here are some questions that decision mentors can use to dig a little deeper:

- Why are you making this decision?
- What exactly are the issues here? (zoom in)
- What do you hope will happen, sooner or later, through this decision? (zoom out)
- Is any part of this decision already made for you?
- Can any part of this decision be postponed and made later?
- Are there any important gaps in what you currently know about this decision?

Listen deeply to their answers, especially if you believe there might be a misalignment between the way they initially frame the decision and the potential to frame it in a way that better aligns with their personality and the decision context. You might use language like this:

- I wonder if this decision is really about …
- It sounds like what you're trying to figure out is …
- How important do you think it is to find out more about …
- What if this problem is actually an opportunity to decide how …

Here's how Javid's English teacher helped him reframe his course selection choice:

> *The teacher asked: "Javid, what's really at stake here? Are you trying to please your parents? Are you trying to set yourself up for a future career that you don't yet know if you want? Or are you trying to explore your own passions and interests while still in high school?"*

> *These questions helped Javid see his decision in a new way. Zooming out helped him shake off the traps he was falling into by assuming the decision was about picking a course and instead look at it from a wider perspective. Zooming in helped Javid realize he needed to have some conversations, first with himself and friends and then with his parents so he could think through what his own real interests were and how they might link to possible education, experiences, or training after high school.*

Framing a decision in a way that feels right can be an empowering way to assert (or discover more about) the decision maker's personality and opinions. If you are talking with a young decision maker about an important choice, helping them align the decision frame with their personality and opinions shows a deep respect for the person they are growing up to be and also the person they are now.

Framing and Advertising

Advertisers exert influence by framing decisions for us. Marketers are master manipulators: they want us to decide to buy their product, so they appeal to our fast thinking by playing with our emotions: *Of course, I need to buy that thing – it will make me so much cooler and I'll have more friends!* Strong emotions – whether they are true to our nature or are falsely created to serve someone else's purpose – are difficult to override. Successfully reframing the choice on your own terms requires access to slow, effortful thinking: *Wait a minute! What do I hope to achieve by taking on this choice?* As the baseball manager (and amateur philosopher) Yogi Berra is reported to have said: "If you don't know where you are going, then you won't know when you get there."

Types of Choices

Frames will and should vary with the type of decision a teenager is making. Being familiar with a distinction among four main types of choices can help frame a decision quickly and in a way that helps it be understood. This recognition of the type of choice makes it easier to emphasize the key points of a decision and, in many cases, also makes it easier to bring in what has been learned already as a result of other similar choices of the same type.

- *Personal vs. group*: Decisions made only by ourselves compared to decisions made in collaboration with others – what shoes to buy versus what to do on the weekend with friends.
- *Urgent vs. relaxed*: There is an urgency to some decisions – sometimes choices need to be made very quickly, so framing has to take place in a matter of minutes or hours. With other decisions, it's okay to be more relaxed and take your time, checking out the opinions of other people or collecting initial information that might help to identify the decision scope or other participants.
- *Immediate outcome vs. delayed*: The consequences of your choice are either visible right away (you achieve your goal – a desired test score or a sales target – or you don't) or delayed (you only find out later if it was the best decision – perhaps much later). Remember that the meaning of words like *sooner* or *later* will vary for each of us; youth have a strong short-term emphasis, so what's "later" for a teenager may be days or weeks, whereas what's "later" for an adult may be years or decades.
- *Stand-alone vs. linked*: Decisions made on their own, without influencing or being influenced by other choices, are stand-alone decisions. Decisions that have a domino effect are linked because they set a stream of other choices in motion (e.g., go to my local college or switch to one in another city). Because they can lack the perspective gained by decades of living, young decision makers

often see decisions as stand-alones. As a decision mentor you can be useful by pointing out the linked choices that are likely to follow. As the great Russian author Leo Tolstoy wrote in his novel *War and Peace*, although it's easy to second-guess the decisions of others, a real leader (such as Tolstoy's character General Kutuzov) never finds himself "at the beginning of some event" but perpetually in the middle of a chain of events. Decisions made today are often the result of choices made yesterday.

Being aware of the type of decision under consideration can greatly help in framing the relevant values and options. Consider the fourth decision type, stand-alone versus linked choices.

Javid may have decided to take band but neglected to consider the linked-decisions aspect of all the other things he would now need to choose, from when he would practise, to what fun graduation activities he would have to opt out of due to his performance schedule, to which post-secondary programs require more math courses. So in Javid's case, he isn't really making one decision; whether he realizes it or not, he's setting himself up for a series of decisions.

One other suggestion. If a young person is feeling overwhelmed by a tough decision, try to reframe their choice so they can focus on a small part of the decision that feels approachable at this point in time. Then help them to choose another small part. By practising on these smaller steps they can work their way into the larger decision bit by bit, over time, learning about the decision context and gaining confidence along the way.

The Decision Sketch

Whenever the best decision frame isn't obvious, it's helpful to run through all the Decision-Maker Moves using what we call a ***decision sketch***. The analogy comes from painters or composers who often make a quick sketch of a landscape or rough out a piece of music before spending a longer time on a painting or composition. A quick sketch enables the decision maker to gain perspective on the best decision frame by quickly working through the other five moves to get a feel for what is possible. It can provide important insights and save a great deal of time, energy, and frustration.

Before starting on the decision sketch, it's helpful for the decision mentor to ask if anyone else should be involved in sketching the decision. If possible, input from everyone likely to be directly affected by the choice should be accessible. Why? Because a decision sketch needs to address the major issues associated with a choice, so it's essential to get the right people (as the "holders" of values) involved.

One of the main goals of a sketch is to decrease ambiguity, so encourage clarity about the words being used. Words like "comfort" and "happiness" might seem clear as things that people are wanting to achieve, but if you poke at them a bit it turns out what feels comfortable to one person – the passenger seat in a car or waking up at 6 a.m. – could feel highly uncomfortable to others. Similarly, what brings happiness to one person may not to another. Whenever an ambiguous or vague word comes up, ask questions like, "What do you mean by that?" to make sure everyone is on the same page. Your main role here as a decision mentor is to ask questions that will clarify the nature of the decision and how it is best addressed. Here are some decision sketch questions for each of the Decision-Maker Moves:

- **Frame the choice.** What's really the issue here? Who else is involved in making the decision? What is already decided and what can you decide later? Why do you feel you should be making this decision now?
- **Clarify what matters.** What is really important here? Why? What do you mean by that? Who else might be impacted and what do they think is important?

- **Generate options.** What are all the ways you could achieve what you're wanting with this decision? Stretch your list of options: how else you can achieve what matters? What other ways might be possible?

- **Explore consequences.** If you go with that option, how would your values be affected? How confident are you with these predictions? Is your information reliable? What would another person have to say about that? Do you know enough yet to predict consequences? What else do you need to find out?

- **Weigh trade-offs and decide.** What option looks best? Why do you prefer that one option over another? Would you really want to give up this for that? Can you think of better options?

- **Stay curious.** How will you know if you've made the right call? What questions do you still have?

A sketch can be super helpful when the range of options is broad or some outcomes are unfamiliar. A sketch also can help whenever the decision maker is not used to exercising their own agency. In such cases, a quick sketch can provide a helpful new perspective on what a choice involves, where it could lead, and what elements remain unknown or might require further investigation.

Asking the Right Question

Gaining insights through a decision sketch is all about asking the right questions. If you fail to ask the right questions the sketch is likely to repeat well-known paths to decision making and, more often than not, fail to highlight new values, generate new alternatives, or help participants learn new things about possible consequences – all the stuff a decision sketch is capable of doing.

There is a famous scene in the movie *The Pink Panther Strikes Again* (dir. Blake Edwards, 1976) that serves as a reminder of the need to ask the right question. Inspector Clouseau is checking into a hotel and sees a dachshund sitting in the lobby. He asks the hotel owner "Does your dog bite?" After the owner replies "No," Clouseau walks over to pet the dog, who promptly and decisively bites his hand. The Inspector is shocked and tells the owner "I thought you said your dog doesn't bite!" He responds "But that is not my dog." Clouseau had made assumptions that weren't true and, as a result, failed to ask the right question.

Sometimes a sketch dramatically changes the decision frame because it brings to mind something important – a new perspective – that otherwise would have been forgotten. And sometimes doing a good job on the sketch is all that is needed to resolve an issue. Remember, a decision sketch is only a first cut. It's okay for it to be messy and incomplete – that's what it's for!

A decision sketch also encourages discussion, inviting questions, and insights. Especially for more complex choices, the use of a decision sketch can be a cyclical process, one that goes through the Decision-Maker Moves more than once because new insights keep coming up. As you help the decision maker work through what matters and what's possible, listen carefully for new ideas or new information that might inform and even shift the decision frame.

Questioning what might be viewed as constraints or limitations on what is being decided can also help youth avoid a decision trap known as **_illusory control_** which can undermine how a decision is framed. Illusory control happens whenever a person assumes that either they or someone else – a teacher, friend, or employer – is more responsible for, or has more control over, what happens than is actually the case.

Illusory control is a common trap among younger people for two very different reasons. First, decisions facing a young person often come up for the first time – no big surprise, since a young person simply has less lived experience. Getting fired from a job can make a teenager think they'll never be employed again; getting dumped by a partner can make them feel a life of loneliness lies ahead. The newness of this decision situation can leave the impression that others have all the power, resulting in unwarranted feelings of vulnerability. Second, illusory control often arises when a young person feels that what will happen depends only on their actions. This can lead to dangerous consequences. For example, if a young person joins a group of classmates in an outdoor activity and feels invincible because they know what they're doing but forgets that others might not, they may end up taking inappropriate risks for themselves or their friends.

Using a decision sketch to help young decision makers realize the limits of what is actually within their control can help avoid disappointment and frustration. It can also help them gain a new appreciation for how much they can do and the opportunities that remain available, despite the presence of real constraints and limitations.

Frame the Decision: For Your Back Pocket

- Correctly perceiving and framing the decision problem means addressing the right set of choices – otherwise a young decision maker could be putting effort into solving the wrong problem.
- As the decision mentor, you can encourage a young decision maker to slow down their fast-thinking system and make sure the frame they

choose fits their preferences and deals with the issues or concerns that prompted the need for a decision in the first place.

- Leading a young decision maker through a decision sketch can realign a decision process. Often, the decision sketch can reveal gaps in available information or a new action that wasn't considered previously.
- Many decisions are better understood when characterized by their type. Recognizing decision types helps in understanding key aspects of a choice and choosing good responses, ones that connect with a young decision maker's values.

Decision Traps

Status quo bias: framing future decisions in a way that encourages the decision maker to continue to choose what has been done before.

Illusory control: the perception that someone – whether another person or group or the decision maker themselves – has more control over the outcomes of a decision than they really do.

Practice

For Parents

Tell your child about a decision *you* have to make and invite them to help you think about other ways of framing the choice. They might find it easier to practise on one of your decisions than on one of their own. Practising this thinking through a vicarious choice will map the thinking process in their own brain. And, by modelling your own thoughtfulness, you are showing them that making decisions well is a life-long skill – one that as an adult you are always practising, refining your skills, and learning new things.

Here are some questions can you ask to prompt a young decision maker to look at their decision in a different way and, perhaps, to see a new approach:

- What's really the issue here?
- What do you ultimately hope will happen?
- What's the best/worst possible outcome?
- Why are you making this decision right now?
- Are there things you can set aside for now and decide on later?

For someone who works with kids, consider mentioning a news story that discusses a decision being made or a problem that exists. For example, you might find a story about something as broad as climate change or as specific as whether or not a new playground should be installed at a city park. Brainstorm all the possible ways you might frame decision opportunities about this situation. Discuss the merits of the various frames. (If you are a teacher, you could even formalize this as a lesson and classify the frames according to types of decisions.)

Go Deeper

- Explore some *Calvin and Hobbes* cartoons by Bill Watterson. There are hundreds of good ones. Calvin and his stuffed tiger Hobbes have a great knack for framing activities in a self-serving and often annoying way that differs from the frame used by Calvin's parents, teachers, or school friends. It's hilarious and revealing, because from Calvin's standpoint he is always right – even if no one else agrees with his perspective.
- Read *Give Yourself a Nudge* (Cambridge University Press, 2020), by Ralph Keeney. This is an accessible book that introduces many of the ideas we discuss in these early chapters. It includes great examples of the importance of framing a decision correctly. With a simple search you can also watch Keeney discuss his ideas online.
- The *Choose Your Own Adventure* books have been a favourite of young readers for decades; since its launch in 1979 the series (originally published by Bantam Books) has sold more than 270 million copies.

Each of the books invites kids to exercise agency and push against the walls of what might at first seem to be immovable barriers. Often the books set up a conflict between what might be best for a lead character and what the reader might prefer. Every *Choose Your Own Adventure* book starts with this advice: "You are responsible because you choose! Think carefully before you make a move!"

2

· · · · ·

Move 2: Clarify
What Matters

After earning a commerce degree, Will got a corporate job and wore a suit to work every day, then came home to a rental condo in the city he shared with his girlfriend. After about a year he started to wonder why he wasn't happy. Maybe if he took more time off or got a dog? But after another year of his job, a bit of travelling with his girlfriend, and a year of going on jogs and throwing sticks for their puppy, he still felt miserable. Will realized he had been doing all the things that mattered to others without knowing what truly mattered to himself. In a flurry of decisions, Will quit his job, broke up with his girlfriend, and moved back in with his parents. That's when he ran into an old family friend, Leah, and, in a rush of details, told her about his life since graduation.

"Will," she said, "what really matters to you?"

"Well, it's not wearing a suit that's for @!*#%&$ sure."

"Ya, I got that. So, what is it you seriously care about?"

Will had been playing his guitar a lot lately. "Music and acting," he said. "But it's more the feeling I get when I'm being creative. Whenever I'm making something."

"Okay, acting, creating, music. What else?"

"The earth. I think we're messing it up and I don't want to contribute to that anymore. It's like that compulsion to sacrifice everything for the almighty dollar – I hated that about my job."

"Got it. So, creating art in whatever form that takes. Integrity and nature – something about protecting the natural environment."

After they identified several more things he valued, Leah and Will brainstormed his options. Living at home without a job was wearing thin. Going back to his girlfriend was off the table. Leah asked Will to start some sentences with "What if I … " and, while he spoke, she wrote down his ideas. Then they talked through how various options might help to achieve his values. In the end, Will made some decisions that others, even Leah, felt were pretty wild: he bought a decommissioned ambulance and, at the time of writing this book, was busy converting it into a travelling music studio.

For now, he has found a way to live independently and make music. It's not the picture of success he – or his parents – had envisioned for his life; but it's a way of living that aligns with his values. And, for the first time in many years, he's excited about himself and his future.

Imagine how different things might have been if Will had been helped by a decision mentor to identify his own values while still in high school. Only after a miserable couple of years spent living his life according to others' values did Will get clear about what matters to him: creativity, freedom, independence, integrity, and living lightly on the earth. In contrast, his previous life pathway was aimed at the goal of being successful as defined by others: job, suit, relationship, dog, condo.

Ralph Keeney (1992) coined the phrase ***value-focused thinking*** to describe a way of organizing decisions around what a person feels is important. As Will discovered, values are not the same as goals: values tell us what matters whereas goals give us targets. Will had achieved many of his goals but still felt miserable because he had neglected many distinguishing personal values. Only after Will clarified his values could he create options that truly satisfied him.

Asking a young person about how a decision might affect the things they care about invites them to take more ownership over their choices. It also focuses attention on the decision at hand: starting with values makes it far more likely that a person will feel happy with the outcomes and recognize that their choices can embody the power and promise of their lives.

We are using the word *values* to refer to those things that matter to us and that could be affected by a decision we're about to make. For instance, Will may care a lot about protecting the planet but most of his day-to-day decisions probably won't dramatically influence this concern. On the other hand, something that in the larger context matters less to him – whether he can stay warm in his converted ambulance during the winter – may figure strongly in his everyday decisions because it is important to him and he has influence over it. The better a mentor can help the young person they're supporting focus in on what could change as a result of the decision they're about to make, the more likely they will be to identify what matters as they decide on a preferred course of action.

Figuring Out What Matters Isn't Easy

Most of us are overly confident we can quickly articulate our values in the context of any specific decision. It turns out that everyone is ruled by their own experiences; we see the world (and the decisions we make) from the perspective of what we have done, where we have been, recent conversations we've had, and what's currently on our mind. This means it's easy for us to be unaware of values that may well be important to us but, at the moment, aren't getting any attention. Out of sight, out of mind. As a result, we often end up focusing on a subset of what really matters to us.

Research supports this observation; one example is a recent study of over 150 MBA students (Bond, Carlson, & Keeney, 2010). The students were first asked to think about choosing an internship program as part of their studies (a key decision for them, leading to career experiences and job offers) and to write down everything that mattered to them – their high priority values – in this decision context. A short time later, these same students were shown a "master list" of values for this specific choice, compiled through discussions and interviews with prior MBA students, and given an opportunity to revise their own lists of what matters. The business students' initial lists typically contained only about one-half of the values they selected as part of their final, revised lists. In other words, half the things on their final lists were not on their minds when they were first thinking about a key professional opportunity.

Half?! Is it possible that we go around ignoring half of the reasons our decisions (and consequent actions) will make a difference to us? Adults often say to kids something like "get your priorities straight" or "think about what's important," as if doing this was (a) easy, which it's not, and (b) something adults are good at, which we're not.

Because it takes effort and thought to come up with a good set of decision-relevant values, it makes sense for decision mentors to

Values versus Beliefs

Values matter when making a decision, because they are important and could be affected by what we decide. We choose to eat this rather than that because it tastes better and is healthier – so taste and health are two relevant values. We choose to watch this movie rather than that one because it's more entertaining and less expensive – so interest and cost are two relevant values. These are decision-relevant values and they are the type we deal with in this book.

Underlying decision-relevant values are attitudes and beliefs. People have moral, ethical, and spiritual beliefs and attitudes that shape their decisions and thus their lives. These deeper beliefs are the subject of individual, family, and even national decisions and lie well outside the bounds of this book. However, we note that these beliefs also influence specific choices. For example, what we believe about how food impacts health will change what we purchase at the grocery; our morals will influence what we find entertaining; our spirituality may change the clothes we wear or even where we want to live. While beliefs can and will vary across cultures, places, and times, they tend to be quite stable and typically influence a wide range of different choices.

encourage young people to practise this skill on simpler problems before launching into a major choice. Making it a habit to discuss things as part of a family or peer group is a great way to help youth gain experience in identifying important values. Keep in mind, however, that moving too quickly to a group discussion, without first allowing time for independent thinking, can suppress independent thought. What's known as ***group think*** can function as a decision bias to encourage *herding behaviour*, where everyone takes the easiest path and falls into line with the loudest or most persuasive voices. Not surprisingly, an effective counter to group think is to have a reasonably good idea of what matters to yourself; as any practitioner of judo quickly learns, it's less easy for others to throw you off base if you have a good grounding of self-knowledge.

Here are four qualities to keep in mind when thinking of a set of values for a specific decision:

- **Complete.** You want a set of values to be relatively complete – taken together, they should describe the main things that matter for this decision. A decision-making process that fails to recognize the multidimensional nature of a choice could increase the roles of misleading external factors. Research on teenagers by Baruch Fischhoff (1996) showed that an overly narrow decision focus could prevent teens from finding good choices and, in some cases, block them from finding any acceptable choices at all. When this occurs, teens are at higher risk of feeling lost or overwhelmed and, as a result, are more susceptible to being influenced by emotional and social concerns that could lead them away from their own values.

- **Concise.** Aim for a relatively concise set of values; four or six values are fine, but any more and it's easy to fall into the trap of feeling overwhelmed. If everything matters, nothing really does. The idea is to simplify the decision down to its most important points. At a later stage, relevant and small missing details can be added back into the picture.

- **Directional.** You need to know, for any value, if you prefer to have more or less of it in your life. That's why the description of a value should include both a noun (stating the concern of interest) and a quantifier (stating whether high or lower levels, or less or more, would be preferred). For example, if you're thinking about going out for breakfast with a friend, you might care about the taste of the food (more taste is better) and how long it takes to receive your order (less time is better).

- **Responsive.** The values a young person comes up with should be in response to the decision they're making, in the sense that the value is likely to be affected by what's being decided. How much money someone has with them today could be changed by their breakfast choice; how much money they will have at the end of the year is unlikely to be affected.

Getting Clear

"Clear is kind," says Brené Brown (2018, p. 48), a popular researcher and storyteller known for her clarity around the ins and outs of being human. Clarity is one of the first things to go if we rely too much on our fast-thinking system. Consider the idea of safety: we can all agree that safety is important with regard to public transit, but we might each define it differently. For a woman, safety might mean good lighting and security cameras on city streets. To a teenager, safety might mean the routes that take them most quickly to their destination. To a parent with small children, safety might mean a tie down for strollers on a bus. When making a decision with others, clearly defining the relevant values gives you the ability to listen intently to others – and it also helps others listen closely to what matters to you.

Here's another common word that has a range of different meanings: success. One way to define success is to figure out how someone wants to measure it. Take Will, for example. Back when he had his corporate job some would say he had achieved a high level of success – a good income and lots of room to move up in the company. However, it turns out that this measure was not one that truly mattered to Will. In the end, he measured success with how much freedom he had and the degree to which he could be creative and play music, so Will preferred other options more in alignment with his personal values.

Will's story illustrates an important aspect of getting clear about our decision-relevant values: for nearly all choices there are multiple things that matter. A student may casually say "Oh, I like that course because it's fun" or "I want that summer job because it pays well," but deeper thinking about the topic will reveal there are multiple aspects or qualities of the decision that matter. This characteristic often turns people off when making decisions, because it takes effort to deal with all the main values that might be affected by a choice: first to identify them, then to consider how each plays out in terms of the relevant decision options. That's why it's important for decision makers to slow down and activate their more reflective side, perhaps asking some new questions or exploring the perspectives of friends, parents, or teachers on the decision at hand.

Asking a young decision maker about what matters to them and understanding why a change in these values could be important to them has three main benefits:

When Communication Fails

A common mistake made by many adults is to believe they are more clear when communicating with others than is really the case. For example, results from a 2010 survey published in the *Archives of Internal Medicine* looks into the reality of how well doctors are able to talk with their patients (Olson & Windish, 2010). The survey compared the perceptions of physicians and patients at several large east-coast US hospitals. Most doctors thought they were doing a good job and more than 75 percent of the physicians thought that patients understood their diagnosis. A strong majority said they sometimes (if not always) explained about the side effects of drugs they prescribed, believed that their patients knew them by name, and if asked would say they are good communicators. What did the patients say? Ninety percent said they received no information about possible drug side effects. When asked "Who is your main physician?" more than 80 percent couldn't give an answer. Perhaps most shocking, more than 40 percent of patients said that they didn't even know why they were in the hospital.

- It helps them clarify their own thinking about what matters.
- It helps them see things from different perspectives, because something might matter to them because it's important to someone else they care about.
- It shows that you (as the decision mentor) care about who they are, how they see the world, and who they are becoming.

Even though something might be hard to define or measure (as with "creativity" in Will's case) it is still important to include it as part of what matters for the decision. If only the single most prominent aspect of a choice receives all the attention, a young decision maker is leaving themselves open to another big trap: ***prominence bias***. Prominence bias comes up whenever a teen pays attention to only the most prominent or most easily justified aspects of a decision, and a decision mentor can help by bringing other elements of the choice back into the picture. That summer job may pay lots of money – but is it also safe? Staying in classes to learn a second language will add to this year's workload, but could it create exciting new opportunities a few years into the future? That second-semester course covers a cool topic – but is the teacher any good?

Another good way to help someone clarify their multiple values is to ask them to imagine an ideal outcome. Let's say a teenager is deciding what dress to choose for their graduation dance, or which computer to buy, or what club to join. Ask them to describe the perfect dress – how they would feel in it, how it would move when they dance. Ask them about the fabric – do they care about how the fabric was made or where the dress was made? Do they care about it being from a local shop or not? Similar questions could apply to a computer purchase: what does the perfect computer do for them? What makes it so great?

Now invite them to describe the opposite picture – what would the worst outcome look like? Why – what would make it the worst outcome? How would the worst dress look or how would the worst computer perform? These are qualities they'd want to avoid.

If the person you are doing this with isn't into writing stuff down, grab a pen and make the list as they talk (like Leah did for Will). Having a visual to ground thinking can be very helpful. And it also provides a record for later. If the computer turns out to have been either a great purchase or a disaster, you and the young decision maker can go back to their list and see if the relevant qualities were included. Chances are some of the things that turned out to be important were thought about in advance but others were not, so the list also provides an opportunity to learn over time about what matters for a decision like this.

Memories and intuitions, often associated more with the heart than the mind, can serve as a source of decision-relevant values. It's a balancing act, learning when to trust our intuitions and when, instead, to use our slower thinking to defend against them. Complicating and informing this picture of faster intuitions and slower reflection is the fact that the line between these two paired ways of thinking is porous: intuitions are often either informed by memories (inaccessible at the time a decision needs to be made so we know something without being aware that we know it) or by statistical reasoning (what began as a hunch is supported, or defeated, by effortful thinking). Consider the following story.

Stanislav Petrov Saves the World

On September 28, 1983 the early warning system of the Soviet Union detected the launch of intercontinental ballistic missiles from the US. A 44-year-old duty officer named Stanislav Petrov was the first to see the warning, which he was required to pass on to his military superiors – who probably would immediately have launched a nuclear counterattack. Petrov was trained to react quickly but he placed this alarming new information in the context of other things he already knew: that the likelihood of an attack on any one night was low, that there was a risk of equipment malfunction (plus the launch detection system was new and thus not fully trusted), and that the information suggested only five missiles had been fired – a surprisingly low number if this was in truth an all-out attack, as Petrov later explained.

What did Petrov do? He made a quick decision to disobey orders and did not report the information to his superiors, which is widely credited with having prevented an erroneous nuclear attack on the US and its NATO allies (a later investigation revealed that the false alarm resulted from a rare alignment of sunlight on high-altitude clouds). Was his decision to not report the alarm the product of intuition or reasoning? Petrov himself gave credit to both, emphasizing his prior civilian training. But it also seems clear that Petrov benefitted from an awareness of the larger decision context and his own self-knowledge, a key element of good decision making (discussed in the introductory chapter), and also from his courage to trust his own well-informed instincts. He was well prepared to act quickly, and this pre-planning for a crisis decision has credited Petrov as having "saved the world."

What about when one of the kids you support comes to you for advice about a choice? You need to balance their values against your own (keeping in mind that the decision is theirs, not yours) and be aware of what your intuitions are telling you as well as what your more cognitive, reflective side is saying. How do you put all this together and have a meaningful conversation about values with the youth in your life without sounding like a robot or an irrelevant adult?

- **For a parent** it might sound something like this: "I know it seems crazy that I get up at dawn and go for a run – but it's really important to me that I respect my body. This is one of the ways I take time and show up for myself – I run. And I notice that when I don't exercise for a few days I find myself thinking negatively about what I am capable of. But when I'm in the habit of running I feel more confident and treat myself with more kindness. I just feel better. I guess the running helps keep me relaxed and feeling positive, and I value that."

- **For a youth worker** it might sound like this: "I get that you don't like me checking in on you all the time. I do it anyway because I value your safety. I want to check on you because that is how I check if you are safe – like if you have a place to stay, if you're going to school, and if you're taking care of yourself. And I want to hear about how you're doing so I can be there for you."

- **For a school counsellor or older sibling**, the conversation might sound something like this: "I don't know whether you should drop that math course. Why did you take it in the first place? Is that a reason you still value now? What has changed? What hasn't changed? Try taking a longer-term view: at this point can you really know you're not getting out of it what you had hoped to?"

- **For a health professional** it might sound like this: "Okay, so you're trying to decide if playing in the game is worth risking another concussion. What is it about playing that you really care about? What's the best that could happen if you do or don't play? What's the worst? Are there other ways to achieve what matters most to you that might be safer and not bring on the same physical risks?"

This is a great time to ask questions about what matters to the young decision maker and to listen deeply to their thinking. Be curious and gently probe to learn more. Then reflect their thinking back to them to make sure you're hearing things correctly. And keep in mind how important it is to serve as an example and to *show how to do* something rather than *tell what to do*. Walking them through how you apply this thinking in your own life models it for them in real time.

Understanding what matters in the context of a decision isn't as easy as it sounds. It's a place where decision mentors can be super helpful by being curious and asking simple questions such as "Why? – Why does that matter for this decision, how might it be affected, and what other things do you think might also be changed?"

Means, Ends, and the Five Whys

Think about the typical decision-making situation we see all the time in movies. A bunch of colleagues sit around a table with coffee cups and computers close by. The boss walks into the room, purposeful and assertive. She announces there is a decision to be made and then outlines the options (either A or B), saying a bit about their pros and cons. She then turns to the group and says something like "Okay, now we have to make a decision." It's rare, very rare (and perhaps not always a good career move) that someone at the table clears their throat and says: "Sorry, but I don't understand. How can we make a good decision without knowing how our values will be affected? And by the way, what are our values? And what about other ways to frame this decision? Isn't that something we should be discussing?"

Hollywood aside, if young decision makers don't first clarify their values – perhaps with appropriate help from parents, teachers, or other adults – it's easy for them to neglect opportunities that could get them more of what they want.

A powerful tool for clarifying values is to simply ask the question "why?" Why do you like this? Why do you not want to do that? Decision scientists and negotiators ask "why?" all the time to distinguish between means and ends: *means* tell the different ways to achieve what matters, whereas *ends* describe the values we really care about.

A protocol called the Five Whys was popularized by Simon Sinek (2011), who attributes the practice to the founder of Toyota Motor Corporation, Kichiro Toyota. Basically, you ask yourself "why?" five times, in five different ways, which is typically enough to get to the core reason for why something matters. It's an especially powerful technique if the first response feels hollow or superficial. The Five Whys could play out like this: *I want this job so I can make a lot of money.*

- Why do you want to make a lot of money? (*So I only have to work part-time*)
- Why do you want to work part-time? (*So I can travel*)
- Why do you want to travel? (*So I can see the world*)
- Why do you want to see the world? (*So I can be more aware of things and make a better impact on the world*)
- Why do you want to make a better impact on the world? (*I just do*)

BINGO! Impact is what really matters here. It turns out that making lots of money was a means to an end. Once the link between means and ends is clear then a host of other conversations, and other decisions, suddenly become possible: How about other ways to make an impact? What about learning more about local problems and finding a job in supporting local solutions, even if it might result in a little less money?

Asking "why?" has another important role to play: it can lead to new understanding about oneself and a better understanding of others. It's too easy to turn off our compassion and curiosity and simply disagree with people who see the world differently. They are wrong and you are right. End of story. However, the Decision-Maker Moves show us that this easy disagreement robs us of possible insights that might result in valuable learning and, in some cases, lead to changes to the decisions we make.

Simply by asking "why?" young decision makers may be able to learn quite a lot about where another person is coming from and, perhaps, realize that the difference in points of view is not so large as we first thought. Journalist Bret Stephens (2017) wrote "to disagree well you must first understand well ... . You need to grant your adversary moral respect ... have sympathy for his motives and participate empathetically with his line of reasoning." At the end of the day a mutual process of asking "why?" often leads to deeper understanding of each other and a new perspective on the decision to be made.

Derek wanted his grade 12 students to do a research project but he wanted them to go beyond the classic "read and repeat" presentation. So he looked for a current story that would impact his urban students' lives. Most of Derek's students used the city bus to get to school. The most common routes were also the busiest and required getting on a large, segmented bus (really two buses, joined in the middle like an accordion) along with a bunch of other people.

As a public transit commuter himself, Derek knew all about this from personal experience. Whenever his bus approached in the morning, Derek – and everyone else in line – would ask themselves (especially if the line-up was long or if it was raining or snowing): Will only the front door open or will the middle and back doors also open? If you guess right (great, the back door opens and I'm on!) you're in good shape; if you guess wrong and line up at a door that doesn't open, then you're out of luck – and may find yourself missing the start of a class or waiting for the next bus (and getting even wetter or colder as the minutes pass by).

Derek learned that this topic – All-Door Boarding of longer buses – has been at the centre of fierce debates amongst citizens and transit managers around the world. Now this debate was hitting the front page of his city's newspaper. Everyone agreed on the core issue: what's the best way for people waiting at a stop to safely and quickly board the bus? But different parties voiced quite different concerns and solutions. The union was concerned about bus drivers being hassled. Riders didn't want others getting on for free by sneaking on the back of the bus. The bus company wanted an efficient transit system, one that would keep fares low but still earn a profit.

Derek assigned his students to create a proposal for city hall. This project meant his students had to come up with a logic for deciding when (and if) segmented buses should allow people to board using either two or all three doors as compared to only boarding at the front.

The decision frame was clear: under what conditions, if ever, should all-door boarding be implemented? His students thought about the problem then got to ask some questions of a panel of city hall staffers Derek invited to visit his class virtually.

Some students created a short survey they sent out over social media. Others polled bus riders during their commute to class. A few stood at the entrances to the school and polled their peers. After a few days they had learned quite a lot about what people saw as decision-relevant values, including needing to be safe, keeping boarding times to a minimum, and making sure that bus drivers were not being hassled.

Their first task was to turn this list of concerns into a concise set of values, using short phrases that consisted of an object and a quantifier (showing direction). Students were encouraged to write these values on the board; after a lively half-hour of scribbling, erasing, and compromise, everyone agreed to the following five values:

- *More safety/security for riders*
- *Less revenue loss from fare evasion*
- *More bus driver protection*
- *Higher positive customer experience*
- *Shorter boarding times*

Derek reminded his students to seek out a diversity of perspectives. So they used a class period to get out to a variety of different bus stops and speak with a broader group of riders, rather than just the commuters and students they had focused on the first time. These interviews brought up an additional concern: ease of ridership for physically challenged users. At the end of the day the class added a sixth value, "Fewer barriers for physically challenged riders."

At this point Derek led them through a quick check:

- *Had they been comprehensive and collected all the concerns that matter? (check)*
- *Was their list short enough to be useful? (check)*
- *Had they thought about the desired direction of change? (check)*
- *Had they only included values that could be changed by the ADB decision? (check)*

The class was feeling pretty good about things. One week later, four students had an opportunity to make a presentation to city staff. The main goal was to ensure that staff understood the range of values at stake in the transit controversy. Any decision made about the buses, the students warned, would need to address these values and show how alternative plans took them into account. Derek felt so proud at his students' leadership and everyone agreed it was more fun than a book report.

Values, Dialogue, and Worldviews

The values expressed by young decision makers are typically consistent with the culture, family life, ethnicity, religious beliefs, political background, and geographic area within which they have been raised. This mental and emotional environment essentially sets the stage for how youth make decisions on a daily basis. A common name given to this larger perspective is ***worldviews*** – the blend of beliefs that shape a person's perspective.

Worldviews help to explain how a person sees their place in society: whether equal opportunities should be offered to all and whether governments should play a larger or smaller role in everyday life decisions. They're helpful because they guide a young person and provide a road map for entering the larger world. Yet worldviews can also blind adolescents to perspectives other than their own. For some youth, the worldview they inherit from family or community feels supportive and helpful, but for others it can feel stifling and rigid and, sooner or later, inspire rebellion. In such cases, conversations between individuals with different and perhaps conflicting worldviews can be prompted by a decision mentor; this support from a trusted adult could be especially helpful whenever young people must make decisions as a group – as part of a classroom task, within a school's student council, or as part of an after-school or community organization. Whether students have a high-quality experience and reach a successful outcome often hinges on their ability to recognize each other's values and relative strengths and to make decisions that reflect and take advantage of, rather than ignore or suppress, the different perspectives and talents of group members.

> Learning to engage in the back and forth of an open dialogue shaped by curiosity will help kids to adapt and make shared decisions in their school, their neighbourhood, and in a diverse global society.

Worldviews are built from core values and, in many cases, the values held by youth will vary widely. Some of these differences reflect cultural backgrounds, others reflect political or religious or economic differences. The influence of these values on the Decision-Maker Moves can be large: some important values might require additional explanation, some alternatives might not be realistic, and some trade-offs might be considered upsetting or even taboo (and hence not open to discussion). Being respectful of other perspectives and values is important for anyone who seeks a successful group decision-making process.

Common Worldviews

Many worldviews can be described by a small number of consistent categories. How people make sense of the world and behave within it often reflects where they stand with respect to these basic worldviews. Research over the past three decades has shown that two distinctions are fundamental:

1. Do people tend to favour hierarchical organizations, where some people have more power than others, or equalitarian arrangements, where everyone has one vote and is equal. Individuals with a more hierarchical worldview tend to trust experts, be less worried about risks, and support large-scale initiatives. People with a more equalitarian worldview are more likely to distrust experts and often question novel technologies.

2. Do people see themselves more as individuals or as members of a larger community? Individualists will champion self-regulation and the benefits of individual actions, whereas people whose worldview is more community-minded will tend to favour public interests, take part in civic actions, and generally support collective activities.

Indigenous knowledge systems inform and illustrate many of the ideas central to this book. For example, encouragement of slower, more effortful thinking is a design feature of many Indigenous meeting structures. Using time and reflection to understand the multidimensional implications of a decision can help soften the initial strong influence of emotions. Author and member of the Gwawaenuk Nation, Bob Joseph (Joseph & Joseph, 2019, p. 88) points out that "it's common for non-Indigenous people to try to isolate certain issues in framing their discussions with an Indigenous community ... . The Indigenous community, in contrast, will likely not consider any issue in isolation" due to the pervasive worldview many Indigenous Peoples have that everything is connected. If this value of connectedness is left out of a decision

82

pertaining to the land, for example, then important concerns will not be reflected as part of supposedly shared choices.

The circle protocol is another example – when members of communities meet in the circle as equals, no one behind and no one in front, with each person's voice heard in turn until everyone has said their piece. Jo Chrona, a Ts'mysen author and educator, observes that "it requires time for everyone to have a say and be heard. It also requires skilled negotiation, a process that demands patience and time, and encourages people to listen to, understand, and consider various perspectives. And while building consensus takes longer than a 'majority wins' process, decisions that result from this have the potential to build stronger communities" (Chrona, 2022, p. 165).

A few years ago Robin was hired by a government agency to help identify and evaluate possible impacts of a proposed large resource development on an Indigenous community. The community was quite isolated, so Robin had to take a ferry into and out of the village. A meeting schedule for the day had been prearranged by email and phone. Robin was hopeful that after morning talks with community leaders and an afternoon community-wide session he would have shared information about the project and, in turn, learned much of what he needed to know about the Nation's main concerns regarding possible impacts of the proposed development on their way of life and wellbeing.

The meeting with community leaders took longer than anticipated because it involved a tour, by foot and boat, of important social and ceremonial sites that needed protection. Then the first several hours of the afternoon meeting were spent with participants asking Robin questions about his work experiences and life, followed by a history of how the village came to be settled and descriptions of people's daily lives. Then it was time to break for a meal. Meanwhile the weather changed and the out-going evening ferry was cancelled due to a storm. So Robin spent that night – with a mixture of excitement, frustration, and anticipation – and the next in the home of a community member. The group met all of the second day and part of a third, with some break-out groups so clans (subsets of the village population) could meet separately to discuss impacts on their portions of the larger territory. It was only on the final morning – after more walks, a long evening session, and many shared cups of herbal tea – that Robin began to hear from community members about many of the expected impacts on social, cultural, economic, and environmental values (all needed as inputs to the project evaluation). At lunch on the third day, the Chief and others explained to Robin that when he first arrived there was no reason to trust him with this information; he didn't know the land or waters and no one in the community knew Robin or his family. It was only after spending some time with residents and participating in the mutual back-and-forth of getting to know each other that community members felt comfortable sharing their knowledge of the area and talking about their concerns and changes to the project design that might need to be made. The ferry arrived late on day three and Robin left, promising to return soon (which he did) and carrying with him a little more knowledge about a different set of values and a different way to meet, talk, and share information.

Collaborative decisions involve multiple participants, such as the members of a class or group, and might require input from people of different ages or living in different areas. Difficult though it might be, this context is also where many of the most important decisions are made. The examples are endless: three classmates who disagree about the topic for a group assignment; twenty coastal communities working out shared strategies to reduce sea-level rise; two neighbours with a broken fence between their yards; four states that argue over a common water resource. Different viewpoints can lead to better choices but only if they are successfully identified and addressed as part of the decision-making process.

One of the key concepts behind collaborative decision-making is the ability to deliberate – to consider thoughtfully and to view something from all sides. It's a cornerstone of democracy, tied to freedom of speech and linked to the content and outcomes of the decision. Being free to speak is of limited value if those charged with decision-making ultimately ignore what others have said to them. Deliberation – whether in a classroom or at the United Nations – needs to be constructive rather than polarizing. In many ways it's the opposite of rhetoric designed to inflame passions and set diverse worldviews against each other; deliberation can be messy but it's intended to contribute to, rather than erode, both the spirit and activity of collective decision making.

Clarify What Matters: For Your Back Pocket

- Listen carefully to help the young decision maker you're supporting to identify and understand the things that really matter to them for any given decision.
- Don't confuse quantity with quality: aim for a complete, concise, and relevant list of values. Keep the number of values small enough that a link can be made from each value to the different options under consideration.
- Remember the Brené Brown quote we cited earlier: "Clear is kind." Clarity also helps avoid a lot of misunderstandings and frustrations, especially if it means a decision maker will avoid ambiguous or vague concepts by articulating their values with precision.
- Aim for dialogue instead of debate. Understanding people's different values and worldviews is key to creating broadly acceptable decision outcomes.

Decision Traps

Prominence bias: the tendency to focus exclusively on achieving gains to the single most important value expected to be affected by a decision, without giving enough attention to other values that also could be affected by a choice.

Groupthink: the tendency of a group to follow the lead of a single persuasive (or simply loud) individual and to miss out on the rich diversity of thought found among other members.

Overconfidence: in the context of identifying our values, being overconfident can lead to the false conclusion that we already know all about what matters in this context – so why waste time talking about it?

Practice

For Parents

- **Make space for micro-conversations.** Encouraging teenagers to slow down can be tough. It isn't as simple as pouring them a cup of tea and having a heart-to-heart (if only!). Making space for adolescents to identify what really matters to them can happen in conversations for sure, but these do not have to be big-deal sessions. Consider having micro-conversations as often as possible. For example, it might sound like this: "Hey I've noticed that you're getting up earlier than normal lately – seems like having a relaxed morning is becoming more important to you." Or, "when we go shopping for new shoes today, what matters most about the shoes you want?"

For Those Who Work with Kids

- **Compare perspectives.** Take a current decision that everyone is likely to know about and ask your class or group or client to articulate what they think is going on in the minds of those involved. This can be an actual, political choice or a scene from a movie most kids have seen. You're likely to hear a variety of different perspectives; encourage kids to talk with each other and begin to understand why their peers' views might be so different from their own. It can be useful to compare their views before and after this discussion takes place, to see how many change their minds after listening to others' perspectives.

- **Learn from examples.** Invite kids to practise identifying what matters to people currently in the news or to characters in the novels and movies they are enjoying. If you are a teacher, you might also have them comment on what seems to have mattered most to historical characters, noticing different perspectives and identifying whose values appear to be acted upon throughout history – in contrast to whose were generally overlooked or silenced.

- **Respect others' values.** Anytime you teach students about the diversity of values, you are helping them develop respect for those who view the world differently. By setting a positive example, decision mentors can help decision makers see how listening without judgment and seeking to understand the sources of disagreement are crucial skills for an increasingly global community.

Go Deeper

- Author and public relations specialist Jim Hoggan has written a user-friendly (and well-titled) book about ways to encourage creative decision making by reclaiming public discourse. In *I'm Right and You're an Idiot: The Toxic State of Public Discourse and How to Clean It Up* (New Society Publishers, 2016), Hoggan interviews leading thinkers about how to encourage more constructive public deliberation and conversations about some of today's biggest issues.

- Daniel Pink's *Drive: The Surprising Truth About What Motivates Us* (Riverhead Books, 2009) is a thought-provoking book. Do an internet search to see animated versions of talks Pink gives about his main ideas.

- Indigenous knowledge systems have a great deal to teach about clarifying values, listening to the ideas of others, and taking a long-term perspective when it comes to making significant choices. We've already noted two insightful and highly respected Indigenous authors (Jo Chrona and Bob Joseph). You could also dive into any of the hugely enjoyable novels of Louise Erdrich (including *Love Medicine* (1984), *Tracks* (1988), and *The Night Watchman* (2020)) or writings by Richard Wagamese or Thomas King, all often read in high schools.
- *Numbers and Nerves* (Oregon State University Press, 2015) by the talented father–son team of psychologist Paul Slovic and environmental writer Scott Slovic is a collection of seventeen essays by prominent writers (Annie Dillard, Rick Bass), journalists (Nicholas Kristof), activists (Bill McKibben, Terry Tempest Williams), visual artists (Chris Jordan), and academics (Robert Jay Lifton, Daniel Västfjäll) about the troubles we face in understanding the meaning of large-scale events and making sense of big numbers. A helpful collection of articles, blogs, and insights – including additional works by Paul and Scott – is available on the Arithmetic of Compassion website: www .arithmeticofcompassion.org

3

· · · · ·

Move 3: Generate Options

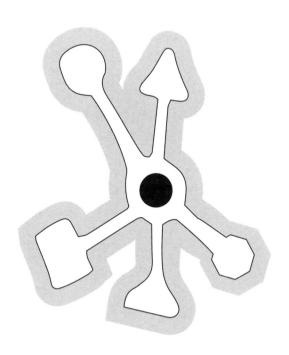

Naya, a grade 6/7 teacher, wanted to do something fun for her class as a year-end activity. Whatever the class did would need to be safe, take place within a 4-to-6-hour time frame, and be free or super low cost. In previous years Naya had come up with ideas for activities on her own. But this year she had already brought decision skills into her classroom activities so she thought, "Let's see what my students come up with using the Decision-Maker Moves."

She organized the class into small groups and set the task: Come up with a year-end celebration everyone would be happy with. Naya asked each group to see if they could come up with four or five values that were important to their choice. After ten minutes Naya went up to the board and each group contributed one value at a time until they had a composite list of class values: lots of fun, highly safe, highly active, low cost, and "everyone can do it" (one student used a wheelchair and another tired easily due to chronic health struggles).

Naya then asked the class, as a whole, to think about year-end activities that would satisfy these different values. One student suggested bowling, something he knew other classes were doing. Another student suggested the water-slide park. Another mentioned going to a near-by nature reserve, and so on. Six or seven options were quickly scrawled on the board. Naya then reminded the students of their values and wondered if any options should be taken off the list because they would score too poorly when considered against their key values. After a short discussion, several options were erased and students began to focus on the consequences of the remaining activities. Ten minutes later a single option had emerged as the clear winner, one that each student could accept and support even if it wasn't initially their first choice.

Recalling this one-hour session with a smile, Naya says the students really enjoyed being part of the year-end party planning. She emphasizes that the Decision-Maker Moves provoked rich conversation and gave her kids a chance to connect around their differences in a productive way. In the end, they accomplished a challenge together – and their agreement created a strong sense of community around the year-end celebration. Naya was impressed but not surprised by the creativity and analytical thinking she observed in her students.

Creating options is an exciting and fun part of making decisions. It's what changes "I have to do this" (reluctantly solving a problem) to "I get to do this" (enthusiastically creating an opportunity). People often excuse their decisions by saying, "I didn't have a choice – it's just something I had to do." But that's rarely true. Decision options are almost always available.

If one young person is about to make a decision, helping them construct options is relatively straightforward. Once they are clear about which values might be affected, they can generate different options likely to satisfy these qualities. If a group is making a decision – a class at school, a group of friends, or colleagues at work – the starting point for creating a good option is for everyone to think about one or more values they most care about, review the aggregate list to see if there are redundancies, then suggest options that could achieve one or more of these values. A discussion informed by the Decision-Maker Moves will keep going back and forth between values and options, generating new ideas but always searching for the option that does the best job of achieving the more important values.

Done well, generating options can be fun and rewarding – especially when a new idea comes forward that is a clear improvement over what otherwise would be done. In many ways, creating good options is the pay-off for having first thought clearly about the decision frame and values. However, too often youth will make choices that reflect their own past habits or what peers are doing rather than thinking creatively about what options could best address what matters to them. Your role as a decision mentor is to encourage kids to put energy into creating better options by overcoming *false constraints* – limitations that can be overcome through a mix of attention and creativity – and by incorporating their own values and those of others who may also be affected by the outcomes of the decision.

Why Bother with Creating Options?

Imagine again a group of work colleagues sitting around a table, discussing what should be done in a particular situation. Everyone talks and talks and as the end of the meeting nears there is the sudden realization that a decision needs to be made, and quickly. So the group makes a decision and chooses an option, some doing so enthusiastically and others reluctantly. It's a familiar scenario: a couple discussing when a friend should visit; three teachers talking about which resource is best; a family discussing movie options. Often the story is the same: talk and talk about different options until a deadline approaches or fatigue sets in, then quickly make the choice.

What's happening here? First, people will often mistakenly consider a long discussion a guarantee of quality. How often have you heard a local government representative brag about the length of time devoted to consulting about a decision, as if more time were automatically a sign of high quality? Not true. An option might be identified quickly and all the subsequent time is merely running around in circles (or taking care of bruised egos). Second, there is often the added pressure of not wanting to appear too strongly in favour of any one solution in case others disagree. Imagine that one of the most popular kids in school (or a colleague at work) is in a group with others who do not rank as high on the scale of influence. They've all been talking for a while about how they want to present a project. Should they do a poster? paper? video? If the most influential group member feels they should do a video, then they'll probably end up doing the video. It can feel like there is a lot at stake socially in these situations.

What's most striking about these common scenes is that the groups typically spend most of their time focused on the different options. This is **option-focused** or **alternatives-focused thinking** – and it's backwards. Without first clearly articulating the values at stake (what matters in the context of this choice), it's impossible to assess how different options measure up.

The common, options-focused thinking approach makes it easy for a young decision maker to settle for a decision that works moderately well with respect to one or two values but achieves nothing (or even leads to losses) in other values. If a decision maker fails to consider some of their key values, then whatever option they select is unlikely to go well because they'll have left out some important dimensions. And if they fail to be creative and consider the full scope of alternatives when making a decision, then those missing options will never be selected – you can't select an option that isn't on the table.

Finding the Best Option Isn't Easy – at Any Age!

Decision researcher Paul Nutt writes about how business and political leaders often fail to come up with new and broadly acceptable alternatives and, instead, settle for options that are less than the best (Nutt, 2004). He describes how most of the senior business managers he interviewed failed to spend enough time and brain power working with colleagues to come up with a comprehensive set of options. Instead, they tended to be overly influenced by what they had done in the past and often overlooked important changes that should have encouraged the consideration of new ideas and values. The managers also often operated as if a decision needed to be made quickly when no such urgency really existed. This "rush to judgment" was often inappropriately used as a rationale for poor decision making. Overall, Nutt found that attractive options were overlooked and executives often failed to select what could have been the best course of action.

Comparing the options against the decision-relevant values *before* comparing the options against one another is important. It doesn't make sense for a decision maker to think about different ways to do something (the options or alternatives) when they haven't yet considered why they want to make a choice in the first place.

Our brains are great at a lot of things, but the shortcuts we take when considering options can sabotage our decisions. Turns out the human brain is awful at considering options on their own merits. Our decisions are more effective when we're able to compare one option to another, as with comparison shopping. Thinking about values first gives us a chance to organize our thoughts and feelings about one option and compare these to our thoughts and feelings about a second option, or a third. We learn what we want to do by comparing the abilities of different options to achieve the values important in this decision context.

The Wisdom of Comparing Options

Chris Hsee, a behavioural scientist teaching at the time in Chicago, looked into how decision options are evaluated when seen on their own versus in the context of other alternatives. In one study (Hsee, 1996), he divided people into two groups. One group was asked to assign a price to

Dictionary A: it was new and had 20,000 entries but the cover was slightly torn. A second group was presented with Dictionary B, which had 10,000 entries and was in mint condition. On average, Dictionary A was assigned a value of $20 and Dictionary B a value of $27.

A third group was presented with descriptions of both dictionaries, and now the relative prices were reversed: Dictionary A was valued at $24 and B at only $20. Why was this? The explanation lies in the ability to compare: whereas the first group was put off by the torn cover, people in the third group evidently decided that the number of words included in the dictionary was more important; therefore, they set a higher value on Dictionary A than Dictionary B. The side-by-side comparison highlighted the more important dimension "number of entries" and, using Hsee's term, made it more easily evaluable.

Remember, with youth you want to emphasize the decision-making *process*, not the outcome. No one wants to always be told what to do. And as an effective decision mentor you are encouraging a young person to use their abilities and agency to come up with several different options that align closely with their own values. If you can help guide a decision maker to use a values-focused process to create options in the first place and then to always compare several different options before getting hooked on a single one, then you've done a large part of your job as a decision mentor.

Our brains are great at a lot of things but it's easy for decision makers (of any age) to focus prematurely on an attractive alternative without asking two questions: how does this align with my values and what other, possibly better, options should I consider before making my decision?

Overcoming Challenges by Creating New Options

Eleventh grader Rihanna is working on an assignment from her career education teacher. The teacher has worked the Decision-Maker Moves into the assignment. This will be the first time Rihanna has thought in detail about what she wants to do after she graduates from high school. Up until this point the pat answer of "I want to be a teacher" has always been enough for any inquisitive adult – but now it's time to dig in a little deeper.

The teacher has framed the task like this: in detail, describe what you plan to do after you graduate. Use the Decision-Maker Moves to help you think this through. Be prepared to explain your rationale for how you handle each of the Moves during a presentation you will give to a younger class.

Since Rihanna had already decided she wants to be a teacher, she framed her decision like this: Where shall I go to college? Here is some of what she had to work through:

- *There's a college in my home town that could work out well, but I'm also interested in exploring other places.*
- *I already know I want to be a teacher and this assignment has helped me see that the subject I think I want to teach is biology. After doing some research (mostly on university websites), I found out I would need to do a biology undergrad degree and then a year-long teaching program or a Bachelor of Education – depending on where I end up going. I made a list of my options – places that have both good science programs and good teaching programs. The list was way too big – fourteen different colleges have both these things.*
- *I decided that being close to home (for holidays) was important, so I added distance – no more than an eight-hour drive – to my list of values. That cut it down to five options.*

97

- *I also realized that I will need to keep costs down, so I had to research rental housing and tuition too. That cut out a couple of places, so I'm down to three.*

- *And I thought of one more value that's important to me: in a perfect world, I'd go to the same school as Georgia, my best friend. She wants to go into journalism, so out of curiosity I added "good journalism programs" to my list. This cut my options down to two places. I'm going to apply to both and then make the decision once I see if I get in. I also might apply to one of the schools without journalism because it meets all the other values – it would make me feel better if I have a back-up just in case Georgia and I don't get into the other ones.*

The teacher reports that the sort of thinking Rihanna shared is much richer than it would have been had the assignment simply been to make a plan for after graduation.

"Plus," the teacher says, "it gives the kids a decision formula they can use if their circumstances or goals change at any point in the future. Their answer at this point isn't as important as how they came to that answer."

As this story illustrates, there are two keys to helping someone come up with good options. First, know that options exist: by exercising their ability to make a values-based choice, something new and better can usually be generated. Second, realize that coming up with good options is not always easy to do.

We're back to a basic distinction made earlier: if a decision is viewed as a *problem*, the goal is to get it over with quickly. If a decision is viewed as an *opportunity*, it's worthwhile searching for a better option.

How can a decision mentor help a young person create better options? Here are six decision-making practices that can help:

- Think outside the box
- Keep it simple
- Be open-minded

- Respect intuitions
- Don't be ruled by past decisions
- Remain patient

Although these practices will sound a lot like common sense (which they are), it's remarkable how often youth – and us adults! – forget about the benefits of possible new options and end up settling for one that easily could have been improved upon. Think of these as prompts you can throw into the mix to help kids consider new ideas and actions – not merely being content with the status quo or what has been done before but instead coming up with one or more better options.

Think Outside the Box

Encourage kids to avoid settling too quickly on an option and just tweaking it. We described this as *anchoring* earlier in the book, a common decision trap that occurs when the thinking of an individual or group fixates on a single event, option, or choice. As a result, potentially far better things to do are never brought up. This same tweaking flaw is often seen in choices made within families.

Dave is the fourth-born child in the family and in grade 8. His older sister and two brothers played on their high-school soccer teams and enjoyed the experience; his oldest brother even earned a partial college scholarship because of his soccer skills. Everyone expects Dave, who is also quite athletic, to follow this same path. It's not really considered an option: you get to the end of grade 8 and you try out for the soccer team.

But Dave doesn't like soccer nearly as much as basketball, or baseball, or practically any other sport in the world. His parents are stuck on the soccer profile and try to be reasonable by suggesting Dave doesn't have to go to soccer camp over the summer, or even that he could skip his first year of eligibility and wait to join the team when he enters grade 10. Dave sticks up for himself and brings up other sports. He even brings up the heretical option of not playing on a team at all. Eventually his parents get the message and, after a lengthy discussion with Dave about the advantages and disadvantages of the full set of options they all agree: Dave will try out for the grade 9 baseball team.

Ralph Keeney introduces this point in his book *Give Yourself a Nudge* (2020) by reminding us that if there are benefits associated with thinking outside the box, then perhaps the box itself isn't the right size or shape. Teenagers are good at making suggestions that go beyond – sometimes way beyond – the mindsets and imaginations of the adults in their lives. If by working together you do a good enough job in articulating values and in being creative about options, then the remade box should be big enough to include creative thinking about all realistic options.

Keep It Simple

Another tip for coming up with better options is to keep the number of possibilities small. It doesn't help if an eager young decision maker comes up with twenty or thirty options then tries to evaluate their strengths and weaknesses. The human mind isn't built for this type of task. Comparing and choosing among a smaller number of options, perhaps five or six, is far more manageable.

It's also helpful to avoid naming the options because naming activates emotions (fast thinking) and turns off more reflective consideration (slow thinking). When a classroom exercise names options after the person who first came up with the idea (Norah's idea or Willa's idea) then it's easy to confuse the option itself with the personality. If the group likes Willa more than Norah, they're more likely to prefer Willa's idea. The same is true if options are labelled as the "low-cost" choice, or the "protect the environment" choice: if we don't pick the low-cost choice then are we saying we like to waste money? And if we don't pick the pro-environment option, do we even care about the planet? Advertisers (and politicians) know all about the lure of labelling options: calling a sugar "natural" or a car "fuel-efficient" can make it appear to be a better option even though there is little evidence to back up the claim. Better to just deal with the options for what they are and see how they line up with and influence the relevant values.

Be Open-Minded

Often, good ideas are rejected out-of-hand by kids because they are thought to be too costly, time consuming, or experimental. As a result, the status quo stays intact: something isn't really working out that well but, what the heck, it's familiar and seems safe. This is a great place for a decision mentor to enter the conversation and encourage a new perspective that might lead to selection of a creative and ultimately more successful option.

Of course, open-mindedness goes both ways. Take the case where a thirteen-year-old wants to stay up well past their normal bedtime on a school night to watch a movie or TV show. When a parent simply says No – "you know the rules and you can't stay up that late on a Wednesday night" – they hold all the agency and are relying on the guidance of an earlier decision. In some cases it may be appropriate for the youth to try opening up this decision-making process and ask Why ("Why can't I stay up late once in a while when there is a good reason for my request?"). In this way they can explore whether it's possible to regain some element of agency by expanding the decision context (e.g., "I know you're worried about me getting that big report completed for school before the Friday deadline. But suppose I work extra hard and get it done by suppertime on Wednesday, could I then stay up and watch my show that night?").

This tension between staying open-minded versus sticking with old habits (or preset rules) often arises when making decisions that deviate from the status quo. There may be pressure from peers to stay with the norms of a group or clique. Youth may also feel pressure from adults to stick with the status quo; this can come up when a teenager wants to make a choice that appears too expensive, too risky, or simply too far outside the knowledge and comfort zone of their parents. Some constraints are real and should remain in place – adolescents are fortunate to have parents, teachers, coaches, and others who care about their wellbeing – but sometimes constraints can be the product of poor thinking or overly active imaginations and fears. At minimum, decision mentors should be open to questioning constraints when they are used to stop consideration of a possible option. By staying open-minded, it may turn out that the presumed hard constraint can and should be overcome.

Respect Intuitions

Our feelings and intuitions play an important role in creating options. Memories and emotions are essential repositories of information about who we are and what we want to achieve (or avoid) through our choices. Influential Swiss psychologist Carl Jung thought of intuition as one of the superior analytical aspects of our minds because it connects the internal and external worlds by concerning itself with "what the external object has released within the person."

We've cautioned that our intuitions can lead us astray, opening the door to decision traps and encouraging an over-reliance on fast thinking. Yet intuitions can also help bring to light feelings or experiences that might not be immediately accessible. Many times a situation will bring up memories from an event that took place years ago. These memories can lead to feelings of fear or mistrust or happiness that take us by surprise. This connection between the present and the past can offer important information about why a teenager might want to either select or avoid an option. Helping young decision makers identify and discuss these feelings is a powerful role for decision mentors.

Don't Be Ruled by Past Decisions

Imagine you are in grade 12, and you're wondering about a future in a construction trade. You have already been working for several summers as part of a house-building crew and you assume that experience helps. Or more precisely – from a decision-making perspective – it *could* help. *But it also could hold you back.* Why? Because you're thinking (as an eighteen-year-old) about all those hours you've put into learning something about construction and assume you should make use of them when, in reality, there are all sorts of other options out there – training to be a chef, a designer, a pilot, or musician – that might actually better suit your talents and your preferences. Consider the time you've put into learning about house construction as a ***sunk cost*** – no matter what you do going forward, your building skills will go with you. So don't let them overly influence what you do next.

The world is full of stories about people who have erroneously allowed the decision trap of sunk costs to rule their choices, ending up unhappy having wasted time, money, and opportunity. An individual keeps putting money into their old clunker of a car (Why? Because they've just paid a $350 repair bill), when it's obvious to everyone else they should scrap it and get another vehicle. A diner vows to finish their meal (Why? Because they spent $11.95 on it), even though they knew from the first bite they didn't like it. A town spends millions of dollars to finish a new road (Why? Because it's already half-built), even though the factory it was connecting to has just declared bankruptcy. In each of these situations, people make decisions to go ahead with something because they want to avoid feeling they've made a mistake or wasted funds. But the lure of the sunk-cost decision trap only means they end up making an even bigger mistake or wasting even more time or money. Far better to admit that, for whatever reason, it's time to change course.

Remain Patient

Even a good option won't necessarily work out right away. Some terrific options take a long time to develop and provide their benefits, which can be a difficult perspective to take when one is twelve. Planting trees is one example. It's a widely recommended way to deal with erosion of soils from land or to reduce emissions that cause climate change. Yet planting a tree requires someone to adopt a medium or long-term perspective, since it will usually take five years or more before that tree really starts to provide the desired benefits of carbon uptake, shade, and erosion control.

Being Patient in Your Negotiations

Negotiators and mediators – who should be experts at framing decisions and helping others make good choices – are familiar with the perils of trying to make decisions too quickly. People often come into a negotiation with very set positions: they know what they want and won't budge an inch, no matter what the other side says or does. A key step for successful negotiators is to take the time that's called for to help move participants away from the inflexible and often biased positions they have when entering a negotiation (think of two angry people getting a divorce) and on to a consideration of their interests or values (the concerns that really matter to them). Sometimes this can be done with both parties in the same room, so that expressed values are transparent and open; sometimes it needs to be done with the separate parties, so the other side in the dispute is left guessing. Either way, an essential part of the decision-making process is being able to patiently move away from an initial, anchored position to learning more about both your own and others' values and then – with help from a skilled facilitator or decision mentor – seeing how these might translate into creating better, mutually supported options.

The former world-champion poker expert and author Annie Duke, who knows a lot about the patience it takes to win big (and encounter losses along the way), warns about losing sight of the long-range nature of decision making. "A great poker player who has a good-size advantage over the other players at the table, making significantly better strategic decisions, will still be losing over forty percent of the time at the end of eight hours of play. That's a whole lot of wrong," she writes (2018). This kind of reality requires a young decision maker to hang in there, perhaps through a series of failures or outcomes that are unfavourable, before they can begin to realize the benefits of undertaking the best option. One way you can provide important support to young decision makers is simply to be there and encourage patience, even when it might not be obvious that an option will eventually work out for the best.

Linking New Options to Values

Thinking about different options requires evaluating them to see if they will help you get what you want. If a kid in your life doesn't know what they want, it's unlikely they will be able to find it. And if they don't directly compare different options, it's unlikely they will choose the best way to get there.

How does this process start? First, they must generate options. One way to help kids come up with a list of creative options is for them to consider each of their decision-relevant values in turn, one at a time, and think of options that will help achieve that value. Once the range of options has been stretched to the max, they can start to combine values and see if any of the options has a good chance of achieving gains on two or three of the desired qualities.

The options that survive this test – that don't have a fatal flaw, in that they only address some values but ignore or fall flat on others – are most likely to be the ones eventually selected.

Let's say your fifteen-year-old daughter asks for advice about whether or not she should break up with the person she has been dating. Things haven't been going that well and she is wondering if it's time to end the relationship. After you stop celebrating (internally!!) the fact that she trusts you enough to involve you in this decision, you could ask what is important to her in a partner. Let's say she responds with these qualities:

- Funny
- Outgoing
- Kind
- Understanding

Great start. Now talk about each of these values a bit more, so both of you can gain a better understanding of what they mean at a practical level. For example, the conversation could open the following understandings of each value:

- Funny: Do I laugh much when I'm with them?
- Outgoing/social: Are they connected to lots of interesting people in a positive way? Do they like to go out or stay in? Are they comfortable in places where they don't know a lot of people? Maybe it's not an outgoing nature so much as confidence that I value.
- Kind: Do they often show that they care about others? What behaviours do I see as most kind?
- Understanding: Do they try to see things from my point of view and not judge me? Do they leap to conclusions before getting quality information and making sense of it?

Next, think more about the list, which thanks to some discussion now includes one more value: funny, outgoing, kind, understanding, and *confident*. Get outside the box and ask if there is someone in the wider world – a fictional character or someone she has heard of in the real world, or someone she met at camp or something – who exhibits a quality she really admired? Maybe she should add that to the list as well.

If you got this far, good on you! You're ready to help her think about the options associated with each separate value. At this point the most obvious options are to stay with the partner or break up, although the goal here is to come up with more options that go beyond these obvious ones. To what degree does her partner demonstrate these values? Is there another person out there who she thinks would better meet these values? If so, add the other person to the list of options. If none of the options feel good at this point, it might be that the decision frame needs another look, further outside the box. Maybe the decision is actually more about how your daughter wants to spend her time than it is about who she wants to spend it with.

We know several parents and teachers who have followed this line of thought and gently, respectfully questioned and pushed a bit to help the kids in their life (with a range of interests and pronouns) come up with revised values-based options regarding suitable partners. One actually spreadsheeted the conversation, *which you would never do* unless the young person in front of you loves spreadsheets. Thankfully, value-focused thinking and generating creative options work well with conversation alone. Active listening is a constant requirement, but spreadsheets are seldom necessary.

Generate Options: For Your Back Pocket

- Get kids thinking about their values (what matters, in this decision context) *before* coming up with options (what to do). Too often young decision makers start by focusing on the different things they could do, bypassing the important first step of identifying why the decision matters.

- Coming up with options is creative work. If a younger person fails to include and consider something as a possible option, then it cannot be chosen. It's that old story about not seeing what isn't there; your job as decision mentor is to help the decision maker put options on the table, in plain view – so they will then be able to make a more informed choice when the time comes.

- People often settle for an option that is good enough – perhaps what was done last time, or what we see others doing – and fail to creatively use their values to generate new and better options, ones that more fully address their objectives.

- Intuitions can often help a decision maker generate good options by signalling that something is missing or some aspect of a choice hasn't yet been brought into play. The task for the decision mentor is to help their teenage child, student, or client to recognize when gut emotions or half-framed feelings are providing a helpful cue and should be listened to as compared to when they are leading the youth astray.

Decision Traps

Sunk cost refers to placing too much emphasis on past actions so that, even if now seen to have been a mistake, they continue to influence future choices among options. Not wanting to admit a mistake or change their mind when new information becomes available often lies behind a decision maker giving too much attention to sunk costs.

Anchoring (without subsequent adjustment) involves giving too much weight to a first impression or a single event. The result is that preconceptions or initial feelings can overly influence and constrain a set of possible options. A better set of options is created when new learning adjusts the information you have on a topic, bringing a richer set of concerns and ideas to the process of constructing decision options.

False constraints occur whenever the set of decision options is limited in ways that really don't make sense because the constraint probably can be overcome. Keeping an open and questioning mind is the best defence against the misleading influence of false constraints.

Practice

For Parents

Play *What If.* Create a low stakes brainstorm session with your kid by stating a value you have and then asking them to help come up with ideas about how you could satisfy that value. For example, if you value improving your health, ask them to help you brainstorm as many ideas as you both can with the following rules: no idea is a bad idea and you each get a point for relevant options. Start each option with "What if." To add a sense of competition – if that sort of thing works for your kids – take turns. The "I want to improve my health" version might go like this:

YOUTH: What if you ate more vegetables?

YOU: What if I started running?

YOUTH: What if you lifted weights?

YOU: What if I started a fitness blog?

YOUTH: What if you entered one of those bodybuilding competitions?

YOU: What if I read a book about health?

And so on ... for this to work it has to be a genuine decision you need to make and you both need to bring along a sense of humour.

For Those Who Work with Kids

Offer kids choices and a template for their voice. Anytime you give kids choice about how they will work or what they will focus on or do (or if you are a teacher, what they will produce to communicate their learning), you can offer a template like the ones collected here to help make their thinking visible while using the Decision-Maker Moves: https://deltalearns.ca/decisions/classroom-ready-resources/tools/

Another good option is to involve teens in choices you need to make, as a coach or teacher or counsellor, so they feel first-hand the power of their own agency rather than merely accepting the decisions of others. This is the theme of an initiative (begun in Waterloo, Ontario) called Teach the Teacher, in which students make presentations (in this case, on the theme of climate change) to the teachers in their schools (see https://youtu.be/ZDGyStq29G1). The intention is to help teachers learn more about the perspective of their own students and, as young people whose lives will be affected by climate change, for teens to convey to their teachers what they feel they need to learn as part of their education.

Go Deeper

- *Ideo* has some outstanding resources about how to come up with new and interesting options through creative thinking and group brainstorming – they're in the design business, so it's their thing. Visit www.ideou.com/pages/brainstorming-resources

- Twyla Tharp, the American dancer and choreographer, wrote a fun book called *The Creative Habit* (Simon & Schuster, 2003) in which she tells stories about her own option-generation process and describes simple activities useful for overcoming habits and the temptation to just keep doing the same thing. Instead, she urges people to trust themselves to be creative and suggests ways to help find a path for coming up with new and surprising options.

- The book *Untangled*, written by the adolescent psychotherapist Lisa Damour (Ballantine Books, 2017), provides a highly readable introduction to understanding teenage girls (with insights and advice often relevant to teenage boys as well). She emphasizes that behaviours and choices a parent or teacher decision mentor might view as unique (Why is my daughter acting like this around me? Why is she choosing this over that?) are in fact evidence of predictable, age-based patterns that may well be an aspect of normal adolescent development and healthy psychological growth. As Damour notes (p. xvii), "Given that teenage girls routinely do things their parents don't understand, it's helpful to have a way to know when it's okay to hang back and when you should step in."

4

• • • • •

Move 4: Explore Consequences

Avery had been looking forward to getting the last pay cheque from their summer job so they could buy a smartphone. They had just turned fifteen and many of their friends already had phones of their own. But Avery's parents made them wait until the end of the summer, when they could buy a phone with their own money and still have enough in savings to cover monthly payments on their plan during the school year. Avery was eager to make a purchase and get started, so they got together with three friends and headed to the mall.

They soon realized that the world of smartphones was complicated. There were four or five different companies Avery could sign up with, and each one offered slightly different plans. Plus it wasn't just a matter of the initial cost: the sales staff talked about reliability and cost and speed and storage capacity and trade-ins and the duration of contracts and cameras and colours ... the list went on and on. Avery's friends weren't much help either: one was bragging about the camera on his phone but a brochure showed that other cameras were really much better. Plus, Avery's friends didn't seem to know much about their own contracts.

Avery returned home disappointed and wondering how they'd ever wade through all this information. Luckily their dad asked about what mattered to them and encouraged them to think about the various short- and long-term consequences associated with purchasing different phones. Avery's dad got out a big sheet of paper and had them organize all the information in terms of things that mattered to them. It turned out that some of the information about consequences was very clear, like the initial cost of the phones, but other information about trade-ins or cameras was hard to understand. And some of what Avery had been told was irrelevant to the purchase because it didn't link back to their values and what mattered to them.

*As Avery filled in the details, the world of smartphones be-
came less confusing. Avery wasn't yet at the point of knowing
which phone to get – they had some questions about long-
term implications of the different plans and wanted to think
more about which of their values were most important – but
they no longer felt overwhelmed. Avery could do this.*

Exploring Consequences, the fourth Decision-Maker Move, is
about understanding what will happen as the result of selecting any of the various options. Or rather, what is *most likely* to
happen. Keep in mind, both uncertainty (about what occurs) and
luck (either good or bad) often play a part in how things *actually*
turn out. Study and do well on the exam, knowing that spending
the evening studying won't be much fun. Don't study and probably do poorly on the exam but have a good time for a few hours
the night before. It's all about the consequences. Eat the fruit
salad or soup special for lunch, feel great in the afternoon and get
a lot done. Choose the huge burger and a double order of fries,
feel sleepy and get less done the rest of the day. Consequences
follow from the choices we make. It's something that parents and
educators tell kids all the time, but how do you get kids to pay
attention?

As you know, the consequences kids pay most attention to is the
stuff that matters to them – and what matters to an adolescent may
not be the same as what matters to a decision mentor. You might
care about making sure they stay healthy; they might care about
fitting in and bonding with their friends. You might care about making sure they have enough sleep; they might care about playing
video games late into the night. Because the Decision-Maker Moves
ground the entire decision in what actually matters to them, the
consequences will matter to them also.

In many contexts, kids tend to pay attention to short-term consequences more than long-term consequences. However, some of the
strongest leadership with regard to climate change and energy

choices, issues that prioritize long-term consequences, is coming from youth. In contexts where you find kids paying too much attention to short-term consequences, helping them frame the decision in a way that emphasizes what matters may encourage them to pay more attention to the full range of consequences.

Identifying Consequences

When individuals make a choice they expect something to happen as a result: order food in a restaurant and expect to eat something you like; go bungee jumping and expect excitement. When a societal decision is made there also are expectations about the consequences: local governments spend money on hospitals because they anticipate lives will be saved if residents have access to nearby facilities. Decisions are made with the expectation of getting more of something we want, or maybe less of something we don't want – so doing a good job of identifying the expected consequences of actions can have a big impact.

All well and good, but what tips can the Decision-Maker Moves provide for identifying consequences? We focus on five key tasks, all rooted in common sense:

- collect accurate factual information
- address what counts
- use multiple sources of information
- bring meaning to consequences
- face up to uncertainty

Collect and Present Accurate Factual Information

Everyone is an expert in their own values (although the younger a decision maker is, the more support they may need putting them into words), but not everyone is an expert when it comes to thinking

117

about consequences and the likely outcomes of decisions. It's not always an easy call: some sources of information are more credible than others, and some people are more knowledgeable when it comes to understanding systems and correctly predicting outcomes. There is a good reason we hire qualified engineers to build bridges, trained electricians to wire our houses, and certified teachers to guide our children.

Research shows that people of all ages rarely question the authenticity of information they consume; instead, we tend to be "truth defaulters" and assume that others are communicating honestly (Levine, 2014, p. 90). This makes sense in terms of evolution and effort, since it would be a huge energy drain if people continuously questioned whether their sources and interactions were authentic. However, online environments such as social networking sites demonstrate a unique set of characteristics that impact the appraisal of information and its accuracy: they spread content faster, reach vastly larger numbers of people, and contain only a limited set of cues compared to face-to-face interactions (which provide numerous nonverbal cues, such as eye movements and other facial expressions). Nevertheless, the reality is that many teens and young adults in North America receive most of their information, from friends and about current events, through online digital platforms. Content creators are thus given ample opportunities to mislead users.

Social media platforms (influencing individuals' choices) and many large corporations (influencing public choices) are heavily criticized for aiding the spread of "fake news" and "inaccurate facts." Although much of their information may be accurate, some is not – and misleading producers and influencers are focused on convincing young decision makers to make choices consistent with a particular political perspective or consuming a particular product. And they get tricky about it, such as describing outcomes in terms of proportions rather than absolute numbers or using highly evocative images that play off our fast-thinking system and shortcut reflective responses. And it's not just big business and politics: letters from charities usually start with stories or pictures of a single child in need, appealing to your emotions in the same way as TV ads for automobiles that show happy-looking models or alluring celebrities at the wheel.

When kids search for information their values and emotions can easily get entangled with the facts, so they are drawn to a subset of what's available (specific sites, certain key words) and ignore the rest. (This is true for us adults too!) The desire for accuracy takes a back seat to taking in information that feels right and fits easily with existing views and impressions. Knowing about the pros and cons of fast and slow thinking can help prepare a young decision maker resist these intentional temptations. We come back to this topic and provide more specific suggestions later in this chapter.

The Perils of Proportions

We noted earlier that our minds are naturally drawn to dramatic consequences, ones that grab our attention or catch the headlines. The related **proportional bias** suggests ways that consequences can be manipulated to appear either more or less favourable. Young decision makers (and their mentors) are easily misled by the difference in a base quantity rather than the absolute number. For example, imagine a presenter at a school function coming out to give a talk on a stage: if fifty people show up in a room that usually holds forty, she will feel great (standing room only!) and the presentation will feel like a big success. If the room had seating for 200 even an audience of seventy-five would feel disappointing (all those empty seats …).

Or consider a program, run by a charity that helps those experiencing homelessness by providing a free meal once a day. Program A reports that, from a base of 500 people, it will feed 400 or 80 percent of the total. This is headline news and the program will be attractive to potential donors. Program B looks city-wide and says that, from a base of 2,000 people, it will feed 500 people – but now the percentage is only 25 percent of the total. When shown separately to people, many will prefer to donate to Program A because it's described as feeding a higher proportion of its base population, even though Program B actually helps a larger number of people.

Address What Counts

When thinking about the consequences of a decision it's easy for a kid to focus on the good stuff, those outcomes that will please them and help achieve something they want: reading that textbook will boost their grade, eating that healthy food will make them feel good, taking that job will get them more money. However, choices usually come at a cost: the book may take a long time to read, the healthy food may not taste great, and the job may be boring or even dangerous.

When decisions are made (especially when made quickly) it's natural to focus first on the benefits, which often have a strong emotional component. It takes discipline and training to pull back, however briefly, and consider what else could happen as a consequence of this choice. Think of the adage *Look before you leap.* Every choice made is, in a sense, a leap. You can picture a shouting match, in which the quieter voice of our more reflective, slow-thinking system is effectively silenced by the louder voice of our automatic, fast thinking system. Your task, as a decision mentor, is to help young decision makers make space for both voices and question their first impulse to extend their perspective beyond only one aspect of a choice.

Use Multiple Sources of Information

Whenever possible, consult organizations and people with accurate, specialized knowledge. Rely on factual evidence about the consequences of the possible options. Many different sources of knowledge exist. Identifying and blending insights from different sources can provide valuable perspectives on the likely consequences of the different options.

Beware of Noise within Organizations

The suggestion to consult multiple sources of information is not unusual; people hearing bad news from their doctor are often told to "seek a second opinion" and shoppers are encouraged to compare prices at different stores. However, recent research has demonstrated a surprising level of variation among employees within even the same organization. One of the highlights of the excellent book *Noise* (Kahneman, Sibony, & Sunstein, 2021) is that organizations often are subject to significant variability across employees, even when the employees are making judgments about the same thing. For example, in jobs such as insurance underwriters, where standard procedures and outcomes are expected, staff estimates of premiums applied to a source of risk didn't vary by 5 or 10 percent but by more like 50 percent – and this was among underwriters of similar age and experience, with access to the same data and working within the same company! The authors document many other examples of variation in judgments and, thankfully, also give suggestions for addressing this surprising (and somewhat frightening) level of what they call noise, such as making sure judgments are independent and using structured decision-making procedures.

Identifying consequences accurately often requires a broad view of what could happen. Everyone is easily swayed by events that are recent, especially if they are particularly vivid or even sensational – these are the same "high drama" traits that encourage interest and media coverage. Ask people how safe they feel taking a train, either when the recent safety record is great or right after a tragic crash, and you're likely to get quite different responses. This is again due to the *availability bias* (described in the introductory chapter) and occurs because our faster-thinking system responds automatically and quickly to powerful and disturbing images.

Checking multiple sources of information can expand overly narrow decision frames, and stretching our initial assumptions by gaining new perspectives is often a good thing. But it's also true that different twists can be given to the same story. Consider an eighteen-year-old planning a weekend trip by car with a few friends. One source might concentrate on the costs of gasoline, another on the benefits of getting a break from their hassling little sister, and others on the benefits of uninterrupted time with friends. Collecting factual information that covers these different perspectives helps round out the understanding of consequences and overcome the (often hidden) biases of those presenting only narrow bits and pieces of information that have been selected to advance a specific point of view or in support of a desired conclusion (e.g., go on the trip or not go on the trip).

Bring Meaning to Consequences

Some consequences are easy to understand, for example a kid forgets to bring a rain jacket and gets wet on her way to school. But often it's difficult to connect with the meaning of consequences. For instance, it's hard to care deeply about the long run, especially when you're young. And as we noted in the earlier discussion of psychological numbing, the human brain struggles to interpret the scope of large numbers. Surely an earthquake that leaves 100,000 without housing is worse than one affecting 400 people, but how much worse? Our emotions don't know what to do with this 250-fold difference in consequences.

The thing is, our intuitive fast thinking system doesn't do math, so it often ignores the difference between next year and twenty years from now or fails to appreciate the meaning of larger numbers. We've found it helps to set the numbers within the context of a story because stories invite our mind and hearts to more easily take in the meaning of an anticipated outcome and factor it into our decisions. Professional storytellers – an honoured occupation, present in every culture – understand well that stories play an important role in cultivating shared feelings, so that the reader or listener is better able to imagine the situation experienced by another individual or group of people.

Bringing meaning to consequences highlights the useful distinction between compassion and empathy. Both terms are often used to encourage youth to care for others and to express this caring in their decisions: we applaud these efforts. However, it's often easier for youth (and adults too) to care about others who look and sound like themselves and are in situations similar to their own. It's more difficult to attach feelings and meaning to information about someone who lives in a far-away country, or is from a different culture, or living in a different situation. As one example, research shows that youth are more likely to think about and be affected by information about the consequences of aging if they have grandparents or frequent interactions with older people (Bjalkebring & Peters, 2020).

Empathy and Compassion

The words empathy and compassion are often used interchangeably by people of all ages. However, in his 2016 book *Against Empathy*, psychologist Paul Bloom makes a case for an important distinction between the two concepts. Bloom considers compassion to be open-heartedness and caring about others and their wellbeing, whereas empathy is a more limited feeling that focuses on individuals similar to ourselves. Empathy comes more from the gut and encourages short-term actions that protect those close to or similar to us. Compassion comes more from reflection and reason and is based on slow thinking: we still feel the suffering of others but we can make distinctions between situations (i.e., an earthquake that leaves 10,000 people homeless is worse than one affecting 400 people) and can incorporate questions of scope and context that are also components of true kindness.

So what? Both encourage taking account of how choices will affect others. Some teenagers will decide that the circle they care about is very broad and includes their neighbourhood, their city, their country, or even the entire world; others may decide their circle includes only their family or a few selected friends. The choice is up to each individual, but decision mentors can play a powerful role in helping their children, students, or clients to understand and perhaps re-examine the implications.

Face up to Uncertainty

The presence of uncertainty also makes thinking about consequences difficult, in two main ways. First, a young person may be uncertain about how they will experience and respond to something that happens in the future. This type of uncertainty relates to values: it's impossible for a twelve-year-old to really know how their values and worldviews might change – over the next three months, let alone over the next five or ten years – so the excitement or boredom felt today in relation to an experience (a trip to another country, a vacation job opportunity) may shift dramatically by the time the event actually takes place.

Second, anticipating the outcomes of actions means making predictions – which can be tough when a future context is uncertain. Sometimes uncertainty exists because an activity is unfamiliar, so we can't really know how the different options will work out because we have no prior experience with them. Sometimes the consequences won't occur until far off in the future, so it's harder to care and more difficult to know how other factors will influence how a choice turns out. This is especially true for youth because, in many cases, relatively more factors are beyond their control.

Facing up to uncertainty doesn't require a young person to become a clairvoyant with a knack for predicting the future. Instead, being aware that often neither the consequences of decisions nor our responses to them can be closely predicted or controlled can help develop resilience and grit, so the outcome of a choice will still be considered okay even if circumstances change in unexpected ways. This insight also decreases the power of the common error known as *outcome bias*, which occurs when bad or good outcomes are assumed to be due to a good or bad decision rather than the product of factors outside the control of the decision maker. Input and support from a decision mentor can be instrumental in helping a young decision maker to first make realistic predictions about consequences and then to live with the outcomes of their actions, no matter whether the consequences match up with expectations due to welcome or unwelcome surprises.

Collecting Evidence

Even though it isn't always easy, it's essential for a decision mentor to help young decision makers come up with at least a rough idea of consequences. Here are several questions a decision mentor could ask to encourage more specific, proactive thinking about what might happen:

- Does your information cover the full range of possibilities?
- Are you asking the right questions to become informed?
- Do you really trust the information source? Why?
- Is the information accurate enough for your decision?
- Is your evidence based on accepted facts or someone else's assumptions?
- What (if any) of the information is contradictory? If so, how will you proceed?
- All things considered, do you have enough information to make a decision?

Any thoughtful decision maker should be at least a little sceptical and will want to know if and when they are assessing consequences based on accurate and complete information. To underscore this point, think about the consequences of the following decisions faced by many youth:

- Is it OK for my health to vape?
- Should I continue to play football even though I have had a couple of concussions?
- Is it worth spending money on a new phone or should I keep using the one I have?
- Should I apply to a professional program after I graduate?
- Should I report my boss for saying/doing something inappropriate to me?
- I'm tempted to cheat on this test – should I do it?
- What after-school clubs or groups should I join?
- Do I tell anyone about a good friend who is self-harming?
- Should I volunteer or get a summer job?

The consequences of these decisions (and many, many others) can be significant. As the adults in their lives, we want the kids we live and work with to develop an accurate and sufficiently complete understanding of what might take place as the result of their choices. But this balance isn't easy: how much information is just enough to make an informed decision but not too much that it becomes annoying or arbitrary? At times kids will feel like they're drowning in a sea of information – this was Avery's complaint when they started looking for a suitable smartphone plan. We live in an information-rich age. Click on a few websites or check an expert's recent post, and you've got what is needed. Or not. When the information we seek is all over the map – one source says this, another that, and a third something totally different – it's easy for a kid to feel frustrated and overwhelmed.

What to do? Once again, adults can model behaviours and provide examples for how questions can be asked and information accessed. Here are some things to keep in mind, in terms of a few essential criteria for the information kids will be using as part of their choices:

- **Accurate:** information that's neither made-up nor self-serving, ideally from a neutral and knowledgeable source rather than a random social media post.
- **Appropriate:** this is partly a matter of precision: sometimes approximate information is fine, but sometimes really precise information is needed. And it's partly how the information is expressed: you don't want the distance from New York to Paris expressed in inches, or the weight of a beagle expressed in tons.
- **Relevant:** information should be pretty complete in terms of addressing both values and context. It needs to speak to you and your concerns.
- **Scaled:** information about consequences needs to cover the appropriate scope and time periods, including immediate, short-term, and long-term effects (depending on the choice) or addressing different geographic areas or populations. This emphasis on scale and scope also invites learning about the consequences of a choice as it might be experienced in other social or natural settings.

Students are typically taught to rely on "science" when they search for information. Science can be a good source. However, depending on the topic and the decision at hand, high-quality information is also available through the experiences, opinions, and stories of people who may or may not have knowledge of science. Perhaps someone is simply a good observer of life and can provide information that's a natural complement to facts provided by science. If someone wants to learn how an internal combustion engine works, they can go online or turn to the neighbourhood mechanic. If a teenager wants to learn about the health of fish in a river, they can turn to marine biologists or directly ask the opinions of people who fish on the river.

Sometimes a specific person is the only source: if a decision maker wants to learn about what's worrying someone, then by far the best source of information is that person. Suppose your teenage son has been coming home late from school; he used to arrive between 4:00 and 4:30 p.m. every day but now often doesn't come through the door until 6:30 or 7:00 p.m. You've asked him several times about what's going on and received very short replies, something about friends and stuff and assurances not to worry. But you do, of course. So after talking with other parents – several of whom tell you they are experiencing the same schedule changes – you decide to talk directly with your son. It's time to gather evidence. You have your conversation, he explains what has been going on and you are no longer worried, plus you've established what you hope will be an open line of communication going forward.

Making Predictions about Consequences

Learning about the possible consequences of a decision almost always involves making predictions about the future – and the future involves uncertainty. It's a hard concept to keep in our minds and our hearts. Very few people predicted the COVID-19 pandemic and those who did were surprised by the range and depth of both personal and global consequences. The pandemic, along with other shifts in formerly stable social and economic trends, shows it has become more difficult to make accurate predictions about such basic concerns as future jobs and career choices or future locations where it might (or might not) be favourable to live. Many days it seems hard enough to make knowledgeable predictions about what will happen next month or next year, let alone providing sage advice about what is likely to happen five or twenty years down the road.

One strategy for making more accurate predictions is to ask, "What can go wrong?" This question helps overcome the decision trap known as the ***optimism bias***, people's tendency to think that their own actions are more likely to result in good outcomes than the averages for everyone else. We believe that our own cars are less likely to break down, our own health will be better, and our own relationships will be happier than is true for the average person. But not everyone can be above average in all ways.

A form of optimism bias common among teenagers, generally known as the ***planning fallacy***, has to do with making predictions about how long it will take to complete a task. Most parents and teachers can easily come up with examples. But let's say a student is predicting whether a big assignment will be completed by the due date next Wednesday. They will naturally start to think about all the ways things can go right, and perhaps respond, "I'd say I'm 80 percent sure I can get it done." Flip this around and ask them to use a different lens to counter the tendency to be overconfident and they might also say, "Yea, I guess there's lots that could go wrong, so it's probably less than 50/50 I can get it done by Wednesday unless I make a plan."

Of course, the quality of a prediction won't be known until you receive feedback about the event in question. Some situations provide predictors with lots of feedback. Think about meteorologists, who forecast weather on a daily basis. If they're not right in their predictions, they learn quickly and make adjustments (or lose their job). Other situations provide far less feedback. If you're in the business of predicting large earthquakes you might need to wait 200 years before learning if your forecast is correct.

Another element is the type of event you're predicting. If a young track star is making predictions about the connection between their training regime and their track times, the short-term feedback should be of high quality and readily available. But if they're wondering about current training regimes and their anticipated health at age sixty, they won't receive much short-term feedback and even after forty or fifty years it will be hard to make sense of all the

129

different factors (including physical exercise) that led to their state of health as an older person.

The bottom line is often trust. What should you do if a young decision maker seems to be putting a lot of trust in an expert you deem unworthy? This is bound to happen as the line between expert and influencer gets blurrier every day. Influencers are paid to impact other people's decisions, especially purchasing decisions, through their relationship with their social media audience. Studies show that in 2019 almost 20 percent of companies in America spent over half of their marketing budgets on influencers. The impacts can be insidious – even very aware kids might not know they are being influenced. So when you, as a decision mentor, notice a disconnect between the consequences the young decision maker expects and your own predictions, stay curious rather than all-knowing. Help unpack their thinking with questions like these:

- What makes you believe that?
- How do you think they learned about that?
- Tell me more about this idea …
- Okay, and what would that look like in action?

If you see red flags around a prediction a decision maker is about to make, it's time to help slow their thinking down. Questions like these can do that. So stay curious and listen.

The Impact of Using *and* Rather Than *but*

In making predictions and working out collaborative decisions it helps to pay attention to use of the word *and* as compared to *but*. Look at the last sentence in the list of questions; now replace the word *and* with *but* and see how the tone changes: Okay, *but* what would that look like in action? Using the word *and* establishes a less confrontational tone. Using the word *but* shows the person you don't actually respect or believe whatever comes before the *but*. Consider these two statements: "I love you but … "versus "I love you and … "See! Now you'll start noticing this tension everywhere! It's especially obvious when someone apologises. "I'm sorry but … " which means, perhaps, they're not actually sorry and instead are mostly interested in defending their upsetting action.

How Much Information about Consequences Is Enough?

Suppose a young decision maker has a good handle on their values and has been diligent in collecting accurate, factual information. How do they know that everything is in place to go ahead and make the decision? That's a big question. Think about the decisions required of people on a daily basis during the pandemic, all the while not knowing whether the information at hand was sufficient to make good choices.

From a decision maker's perspective, more information is of value to the extent that it changes the decision to be made. Whether the average daily temperature at a place you want to visit varies by a couple of degrees doesn't much matter, so getting the latest weather updates probably isn't necessary. But if the temperature range varies by twenty or so degrees, the value of this information is higher because the greater temperature difference may change the decision you make about going to this place (or at least what you'll want to bring with you).

Lots of factors can affect whether the information at hand is sufficient to make a decision. If you're standing outside a burning building and need to decide whether you can safely make one more trip inside to rescue the family photos, it's not the time to pull out pencil and paper and start evaluating different scenarios. Even so, having the practised logic of the Decision-Maker Moves in the back of your mind is helpful.

This question "Is there enough information to decide?" comes up all the time, from minor decisions right up to significant social choices. On the one side, think about going to a restaurant for the first time and ordering your dinner. The menu will have short descriptions of each food item, but often you need to ask questions to gain more information: Is the fish grilled or fried? Are the strange-sounding vegetables served hot or cold? What's the soup of the day? Does the salad have nuts? You ask a few questions and, when you feel comfortable enough (and hopefully before you begin to sound like a complete jerk), you go ahead and order. And if there are still some surprises when the meal arrives it's not a big deal. It's only one meal and tomorrow is another day.

On the other side, think about the information government needs to make accurate forecasts of incoming funds from taxes or the benefits of making large outlays for infrastructure projects like bridges or highways. Such decisions are often partly based on predictions about future trends – how many more people will be moving into an area, and where will they most likely be living, working, and shopping? Elected officials are asked to make decisions like this all the time, and they may keep or lose their jobs based on the quality of the choices they make with incorrect or incomplete information regarding the consequences of their actions.

Scaling up to National Policies

Co-author Robin has worked with senior military leaders on ways to improve their decision-making skills. One group of senior military officers, focused on the threat to national security posed by domestic and foreign terrorists, used the Decision-Maker Moves to help inform a series of difficult (and potentially very significant) choices about how best to improve national security.

As part of a two-day workshop, participants were given a realistic but hypothetical scenario dealing with a likely terrorist threat and asked what they thought would be an appropriate response. Some participants argued that the information at hand was sufficient to favour an immediate strike, designed to heavily damage the terrorist group's headquarters. Others suggested a wait-and-see attitude, keeping close surveillance on the group's activities. It turns out, this difference in choices hinged on an evaluation of the quality and extent of recent intelligence information, which everyone agreed was spotty but also worrisome in terms of the possible consequences of terrorists' actions. The wait-and-see participants also questioned whether a leading source of information might itself be biased, so they saw this as another reason to wait and try to learn more.

The group discussed what to do well into the second evening – just as a decision mentor might do with a kid they care about – trying to figure out if they were sufficiently comfortable with the available information to go ahead and make a potentially fateful decision. At the end of the session a decision was made to gather more information from new sources, largely due to a lack of trust in the key source and a realization that a short delay would not greatly increase the risk level.

Usually there is no clear bottom line concerning the sufficiency of information. It's a judgment call, with the avoidance of regret figuring strongly in the picture. However, asking a few simple questions can often provide useful insights:

- How much factual uncertainty exists: lots? only a little?
- How significant is the information gap's consequence on the choices to be made?
- What might be learned by waiting until new information becomes available?
- How much urgency is there: is it likely that waiting a short time would cause serious problems?
- Is this a one-time choice or could it be split up into a series of choices, some to be made now and some later?

Distinguishing Accurate from False Information about Consequences

As a decision mentor, you can help a young person locate reliable information sources to help predict what will probably take place. However, in the past decade or two it has become more difficult to figure out fact from fiction because often facts become entangled in polarized values. What's to be done? Here are some reminders you can offer decision makers:

- **Rhetoric:** Notice the way a person sounds and the words they use: do the vibes they give off seem inflammatory? angry? extreme?
- **Diversity:** Is the source expressing only one point of view or a range of views? Is one point of view dominant or are all voices being listened to?
- **Plausibility:** Is what is being said likely to be possible and accurate, given what you know up to this point? If not, this can trigger a more sceptical, questioning approach.
- **Funding:** If something is written by a member of an organization, check out the group and see where their funding comes from. Sometimes hidden or obvious motivational biases exist, resulting in tweaks to information collection processes to please funders.
- **Biases:** Ask yourself whether opinions might be subject to decision biases, such as anchoring on a single event or emphasizing only one dimension of a more complex choice.
- **Noise:** Collecting information usually requires judgments – about what sources to trust or about how much importance to assign what is found out. These choices-within-a-choice are often subject to surprising variability, both within a person (e.g., on different days) and among different people – so an element of noise is often present when collecting information.

- **Online fact checkers** can be a big help in examining the truth of so-called facts dealing with politicians and different public policy initiatives (for example: FactsCan.Ca in Canada, FullFact.org in the UK, or FactCheck.org in the US).

People of all ages tend to be highly influenced by the source of information and whether the person delivering a message is seen as credible and trustworthy. Trust levels in many sources of information, and in particular government and industry leaders, have declined in recent years. This same period has seen tremendous growth in internet and social media use. Unfortunately, we often don't get unfiltered information from social media feeds because algorithms reinforce what we already believe. Think of the first items you see when Googling a topic; where on the page the results show up depends on the type of information we've searched for in the past and who is paying to manipulate the algorithm with sponsored content. When co-author Robin Googles "mindfulness" his list is topped by research and news articles connecting mindfulness to wellbeing. When Brooke searches "mindfulness" she gets yoga retreats, meditations, and therapy ads. Try searching "turkey" and see what comes up. News articles about Turkey's political context? Vacation information for those going to Turkey? Soup and dinner recipes featuring turkey?

The impact of this sorting means it's easy to end up in a bit of an echo chamber. This is the decision trap known as ***confirmation bias***, where the information we pay attention to only serves to reinforce our existing point of view. It is less that we are *informed* by information, open to surprises and new insights, and more that we are *affirmed* and, too many times, end up more convinced of our earlier point of view.

The Problematic Confirmation Bias

Confirmation bias describes the tendency people have to embrace information that supports their position and reject contradictory information. Anyone who has watched or listened to the news over the past several years will be aware of this commonplace bias, which has been the subject of extensive study (along with its potential cures). A classic early study involved a group of university students with opposing opinions about capital punishment: half were in favour and thought it would reduce crime while the other half were opposed and thought it had no effect on crime (Lord, Ross, & Lepper, 1979). Two reports were given to all the students, one with statistics supporting the deterrence argument and the other with facts calling it into question – unbeknownst to the students, both articles were made up. Those in support of capital punishment rated the study supporting their deterrence position as highly credible and the other study as unconvincing; as you may by now have guessed, the students opposed to capital punishment did the reverse. The disturbing moral is that, after being exposed to a range of views, these young adults did not become more sceptical or curious about their beliefs but, instead, found reasons to become even more strongly aligned with their initial position.

Thankfully facts alone don't make choices, people do. Decisions always reflect facts and values. An expert, a website, or a trusted friend may be terrific at providing factual information about the effects of an action, but that person won't know what you want because they don't know you or your values. Accurate factual evidence is useful (and necessary) because it informs young decision makers about possible changes in things that matter. Ultimately a decision will be made based on how an individual, a family, a group, or a nation's citizens feels about the consequences that matter most to them.

Is It Wise to Trust an Expert?

No matter what the topic, when it comes to considering the consequences of options, a frequent question asked by teenagers is, "Who should I ask about this?" Selecting a reliable source of expertise is challenging right now. The polarization of views and sharp differences in people's opinions can mean that what is safe to one expert is dangerous to another.

Some of us turn to famous personalities for guidance, even if the topic in question is one the celebrity knows little about. Some of us will only trust a certified plumber and will only accept medical help from a medical doctor. Others equate expertise with having done something for a long time: I'll trust my uncle when it comes to plumbing because he built his own house and everything works. The bottom line to keep in mind is that who you (as an adult) view as an expert might differ from who a young person sees as an expert and, perhaps, how they define expertise.

The frequent divergence between experts' predictions about the future and what actually happens has prompted many people to question whether there really are *any* experts out there. The most famous examples of experts failing to make accurate predictions are probably political opinion polls. Candidates predicted to "win in a landslide" lose more often than expected, and individuals given "a very low chance" of success come through and end up on top. The same is true in sports: a group of seemingly well-informed sports reporters sit around a TV studio and tell us why Team A is going to dominate Team B in the upcoming game, and then scramble to explain why Team B ends up winning the game (and why they secretly knew all along that this would happen).

Psychologist James Shanteau asked "Where are the true experts?" as part of a study that examined which disciplines have experts and which do not (Shanteau, 1992). Shanteau was looking for regularity: what are the professions whose spokespersons are able to make reasonably good predictions? The results are disconcerting. Experts who tend to be most knowledgeable are in fields such as accounting, astronomy, games like chess or poker, or photo interpretation. Unfortunately, the experts whose predictions are often wildly wrong include disciplines where most people typically want to rely on expert advice: stockbrokers, college admission officers, intelligence analysts, psychiatrists, and court judges. Yikes!

Adding to these difficulties in identifying and trusting experts is the fact that experts themselves, being human, can be biased. One source of bias is a person's motivation: asking questions such as "Who is paying for this information?" or "Did the expert giving the advice have anything to gain by saying what they did?" can help identify bias. Another source goes back to the decision trap of anchoring – giving too much attention to what happened last week or last month. Studies of scientific experts support this dismal point of view: biologist Mark Burgman found that scientists' predictions were accurate less than one-half the time and in many cases were no better than guesses (Burgman, 2016). Experts are naturally overconfident: once someone is called an expert it's less likely they will question themselves ("Why should I have doubts? I'm an expert!"). It's then easy for the person and the larger world to believe that the acclaimed expert's knowledge is accurate and of great value. So the definition of an expert helps create overconfidence.

The Consequence Table: A Powerful Organizing Tool

The main purpose of a consequence table is to offer a user-friendly, visual tool for matching information about what matters to the decision maker with the consequences of different options. It's a powerful tool decision mentors can use to cut through a decision makers' feelings of confusion about difficult decisions they face. Once adults have shown younger decision makers how to use a consequence table, kids can easily use the tool on their own (as we've seen in elementary and high schools).

Consequence tables work in the same way as bookshelves or closets. Imagine a messy bedroom, with clothes, games, books, and shoes thrown helter-skelter all over the floor, the bed, and a chair. It's not a pretty sight. But then you get a cabinet or closet shelf with places for everything and order appears out of the chaos. That's what a consequence table does for decision making: it's a simple and elegant visual tool for organizing several of the Decision-Maker Moves in a way that makes them easy to apply to decisions.

A consequence table has three main components.

- Along the left side you list decision-relevant values: what matters in the context of this choice (and note whether you want more or less of the value).
- Across the top you list options, the different ways to achieve the values.
- In the cells, you note the likely consequences of each option in terms of the impacted values.

Decision goes here	Option 1	Option 2	Option 3
Value 1	How well Option 1 satisfies Value 1	How well Option 2 satisfies Value 1	How well Option 3 satisfies Value 1
Value 2	How well Option 1 satisfies Value 2	How well Option 2 satisfies Value 2	How well Option 3 satisfies Value 2
Value 3	How well Option 1 satisfies Value 3	How well Option 2 satisfies Value 3	How well Option 3 satisfies Value 3

Read across the rows and see how each option varies in terms of a single value; read down the columns and see how each option measures up in terms of the various values. You'll see an example filled in below.

Simple and beautiful, the logic of the consequence table can unlock a wealth of insights. A good consequence table shows how the different options stack up against each other and what matters. It simplifies the decision, makes consequences more clear, and helps the decision maker cut through to what matters.

Four friends are buying tickets online for a performance of their favourite group, which is coming to town in about two months. The venue is the large indoor stadium downtown, used by the local pro soccer team during their season. The friends need to make a decision about what tickets to purchase, and quickly: tickets go on sale the next night at 10 pm and are expected to sell out within the first hour.

Everyone meets up at Sam's house after dinner to figure it out. Tracy wants to make sure they don't cheap out because she wants to get up close and have a good view; her favourite musician in the world is the group's drummer. Alain, recently laid off from his after-school job, is worried about cost. Zoe is anxious about getting to the concert on time because she has the longest commute; Sam is on crutches from a recent skateboarding injury and will most likely still have trouble walking in a couple months, so they worry about where they're going to sit.

If the four friends had decided to use a consequence table it might have looked like this.

Values	Option A: in front of stage	Option B: bleachers	Option C: middle
Better view	excellent	good	good
Lower cost	$$$$	$	$$
More comfort	fine	fine	fine
Later arrival	90 minutes	60 minutes	75 minutes

The consequence table helps simplify and clarify what previously felt a little chaotic and overwhelming. The friends would now see that Option B is the same as or better than Option C for all four values. For Zoe the difference between arriving 60 and 90 minutes ahead of the start time for the concert isn't a big deal. So they would agree this concern doesn't really affect the decision.

Bringing in these two observations – the dominance of Option B over C and the irrelevance (for this decision) of differences in arrival times – means that the final consequence table can be simplified. The final consequence table now shows only two options and two values. Everyone's views have been explored but the final decision is now much simpler: is it worth spending the extra money on tickets to (probably) end up with a better view?

Values	Option A: in front of stage	Option B: bleachers
View	excellent	good
Cost	$$$$	$

Does the consequence table tell Tracy, Sam, Alain, and Zoe what to do? No. It provides insights, not answers. Their decision will also depend on the importance assigned to each of the values: Tracy really wants to be up close to the stage whereas Alain is worried that if tickets cost too much, he won't be able to go. The different values won't be equally important when it comes to making a choice and there may need to be some negotiations among the friends (can anyone cover part of Alain's ticket?). We'll talk more about dialogue and trade-offs later.

A consequence table is a simple and valuable organizing tool that can bring a great deal of insight to decision makers and provide a visible, easy-to-follow map for discussing the consequences of different options.

Using a Consequence Table with Youth

Remember in Move 2 when Will was talking to Leah about his frustration and confusion around what he should do next with his life? Because Leah knew the logic of the Decision-Maker Moves, she quickly sketched a table in her mind – which you'd now recognize as a consequence table – while he spoke, enabling her to think visually about what Will was saying. Once put down on paper, he was better able to think about what mattered to his choices.

This is obviously an ideal situation – Leah knew the Decision-Maker Moves pretty well and Will was open to having his thinking put into a matrix. The scenario you find yourself in might be different. Regardless, when a young decision maker feels overwhelmed like Will was, a decision mentor who listens deeply and asks questions can be a huge help, resulting in more clarity about what is at stake and what can be done. This expression of compassion and comfort is embedded in the Decision-Maker Moves. The Moves provide a map for what writer Ram Dass said of such conversations: "We're all just walking each other home" (www.ramdass.org).

Leah did exactly that – first listening to Will, then "walking him home" as she helped organize his thinking. In a classroom or with a large group of decision makers, the same can be true. Start out with a free and open conversation. Then when things start to go around in circles, or people focus prematurely on one option, introduce the consequence table to pull the conversation together and move to a decision before there is a group meltdown due to frustration or overwhelm. In particular, consequence tables help keep young decision makers focused on the task of generating and comparing options rather than closing down and insisting that their favourite option is the best and only choice. A little organization goes a long way.

Explore Consequences: For Your Back Pocket

- Consequences are why we care about decisions. When we like the consequences of a decision, we're pleased. When we don't like the consequences, we're unhappy. It pays to get clear about the consequences associated with various options.
- Collecting accurate, unbiased information about the consequences of actions ensures the decision maker is dealing with reality. But not all information is helpful: if learning something additional won't change the decision that's being made, then the value of the information is very low.
- Determining who is considered an expert, and the extent to which their expertise is considered credible, can vary greatly across people. In today's world of omnipresent social media and well-paid influencers, it can be misleading to believe information as presented unless you ask tough questions about its source, relevance, and accuracy.
- Not all consequences matter the same amount; some are of little importance whereas others may be life-changing. Not all consequences are equally likely: some outcomes are almost certain to take place but others less so.
- A consequence table organizes thinking and brings additional clarity to decisions. It's most useful as a reminder of the logic and key points needed to help organize a decision-making process.

Decision Traps

Confirmation bias is when we look to confirming evidence and ignore contradictory information. Many observers argue that confirmation bias lies behind much of the polarization in society, with many of us turning to social media and newscasts that support our point of view and filter out disconfirming evidence – information designed to affirm what already is believed rather than to inform.

Outcome bias occurs when a bad outcome is assumed to be due to a bad choice or a good outcome is assumed to be due to a good choice. This common decision error omits the role of external factors – all the other things that are going on outside the control of the decision maker – and also the role of bad or good luck.

Optimism bias occurs when we believe that things will turn out well for us and that we, and those we know, will be less subject to bad events. Things such as auto accidents, sickness, badly timed snowstorms, or getting caught for minor misbehaviours will happen to others, not to us. One form of this bias is that we tend to be overly optimistic about how quickly tasks will be completed; the existence of this "planning fallacy" is well known among parents of teenagers who face deadlines on completion of their school projects.

Proportional bias is based in ways that our brains interpret consequences expressed as proportions rather than as absolute numbers in order to manipulate information to appear more or less favourable. Young decision makers (and their mentors) can easily be misled by the proportional difference in a base quantity rather than the absolute numbers.

Practice

For Parents

- **Practise curiosity.** The next time you find yourself telling your child what will happen if they don't eat their vegetables, clean their room, study for a test, or write thank you notes, stop. Rather than tell them, ask them. It might sound like this: "I see you're playing a lot of video games every afternoon. What do you think are the impacts of doing that?" If you do this, remember not to use a *tone*. This is not meant to be a passive-aggressive way to have them parrot what they think you think the consequences are. Get genuinely curious about what the impacts are from your child's perspective. You will learn something and you'll also help your child learn a new thinking pattern.

- **Model decisions.** Think of a decision you need to make. Sketch it out in a consequence table. Then ask your child to help you flesh it out even more. Ask them to be the question asker – helping you make sure you've thought it all through. This approach is powerful because making yourself vulnerable in this way helps build trust between you and your child. You will be showing them that you respect their thinking and value their contribution. And you will be walking them through the style of thinking you want them to use when faced with their own decisions.

For Those Who Work with Kids

- **Make your rationale for trusting expertise explicit.** If you are sharing information, share your source and also why you trust the source. This detail is particularly important given the amount of misinformation out there.
- **Practise using a consequence table.** Whether virtual or physical, on paper or a computer screen, it can be helpful to show your thinking in a consequence table. Used as a decision aid, the consequence table can be a simple way to help a decision maker focus their thinking about objectives, options, and the different consequences of their choices. It helps the decision maker see their choice from a more holistic vantage point, making it easier to look at their thinking and review it for gaps.
- **If you are a teacher, try a different take on the "Two truths and a lie" game.** A fun game that teachers sometimes play when getting

145

to know a new class has each person tell two truths and one lie about themselves. The rest of the class then guesses which is the lie.

- On a similar theme, assign pairs of students to create 30-second information pieces that could be shared on a social media platform. Working in pairs from a list of topics you provide of an idea of their own, have one person in each pair create the piece using true information and one using false information. Each pair would then present to the full class, or to another class in the school. The audience would be tasked with distinguishing the truth from the lie. With your facilitation, rich discussion around what criteria they used to make their decision will ensue. This simple game is instructive, showing (among other things) how disarmingly simple it can be to create misleading yet believable information and how insight, clear thinking, and probing questions – all of which require slow thinking and effort – can often expose misleading information.

Go Deeper

- For those wanting to understand the factual side of consequences, a helpful book is *Naked Statistics*: *Stripping the Dread from the Data* (Penguin Random House, 2012). In this bestseller, author Charles Wheelan grabs from business, sports, politics, advertising, and many other areas to illustrate how statistics are used to inform, misinform, and even delight the modern decision maker.
- An excellent source of training for young social media users is a site out of Cornell University called Social Media Test Drive: https://socialmediatestdrive.org/for_parents.html. The goal of the site is to train young adults to become better, more savvy consumers of social media information; it's designed as a stand-alone that youth can complete on their own and it also encourages parents and teachers to use the site's resources to teach kids about the promise and perils of social media.

- Check out this blog post about how to tell fact from fiction using a handy acronym called SIFT: https://hapgood.us/2019/06/19/sift-the-four-moves/

- TV producer and educator Brett Pierce has written a short and helpful book titled *Expanding Literacy: Bringing Digital Storytelling into Your Classroom* (Heinemann, 2022) on digital storytelling. It builds on Brett's *Meridian Stories* website and provides examples of ways to prepare youth for living in a digital world, with exercises designed to increase student agency and understanding that can easily be adapted by parents and teachers.

- *Noise: A Flaw in Human Judgment,* by Daniel Kahneman, Olivier Sibony, and Cass Sunstein (Little, Brown Spark, 2021), provides numerous examples of ways in which human judgments are subject to surprisingly wide variations, both within and among people. Evidence comes from the disturbing differences in the choices made by groups of business leaders, lawyers, and doctors (as well as young adults, parents, and teachers) who make very different decisions despite having access to identical information.

5

· · · · ·

Move 5: Weigh Trade-offs and Decide

Malala Yousafzai won the Nobel Peace Prize when she was seventeen. In part, the world knows about her because when the Taliban prohibited girls from attending school in Afghanistan, she spoke up about it, writing articles and giving talks. As is clear by her writing, Malala has strong values that include justice and equality for women as well as a love of learning and education. She also values safety. In making her choice to speak up and criticize her government's decision, Malala was aware that she was increasing risks to herself and her family. In response, the Taliban shot (then fifteen-year-old) Malala in the head while she was on a school bus. Thankfully, she survived and continues to advocate for a future where girls are free to learn and lead.

Malala made decisions based on trade-offs among her values, even when the priority she placed on equality and justice made her vulnerable to Taliban hostility and increased her own risk of death. She quite literally decided to stand up and identify herself on the fateful day when the Taliban boarded her bus and demanded that she do so. Malala has said that, in that instant, she was willing to trade her life for the freedoms she valued. Through ongoing work with her foundation, the Malala Fund, her story continues to inspire millions of people to create a more just and equitable world.

Malala's decision makes for such a powerful story because it holds up a mirror, prompting us to consider what would we be willing to put on the line in order to remain true to our values? Few of us are required to make values-based decisions involving issues of life and death. Most decisions are not so extreme. However, on another level, today's youth *are* making life and death decisions regularly, and often very quickly – which is why, as part of our earlier discussion, we emphasized the importance of thinking ahead and using some of the Decision-Maker Moves in advance so you have an immediately available approach to deal with the situation.

The contexts for these life-and-death decisions are varied and usually won't involve facing armed men on a bus. But if a thirteen-year-old is at a party and is offered an unfamiliar pill, then they could well be making a life and death decision. If a fifteen-year-old is thinking about becoming sexually active, that decision could forever open some options and close others. If an eighteen-year-old is considering whether to cheat on a test, the implications of such a decision could be far-reaching.

Making trade-offs can be tough: each of these choices requires balancing across a range of gains and losses, emotions and reflections. We want many things and we can't have them all. We exercise to remain healthy, but don't like to get exhausted; we want to eat out at a restaurant, but can't spend too much money; we care about saving an endangered species, but don't want to deny people recreational access to its habitat; we seek to collaborate with classmates on a project, but want to avoid constant meetings; we tried to stay safe during the COVID-19 pandemic, but also wanted to get out and have fun. These are all choices that force us to identify and address trade-offs.

There is perhaps no better way to get clarity around what really matters than when you have to give something up in order to achieve what you want. In this way, young decision makers can define who they are by articulating and making trade-offs in an intentional and thoughtful way. It follows that a reasonable consistency in making trade-offs is important. Coaches aren't happy with players on a school team who try super hard one week but slack off the next; essentially, the players are making different trade-offs week-to-week and the coach doesn't know what to expect.

Trade-offs require finding a balance among the consequences of different actions. Our choices, when well thought out and deeply intentional, reveal something fundamental about who we are.

Why Are Trade-offs Difficult?

During his years as President of the United States, Barack Obama had a plaque hanging on the wall of the Oval office that said *Hard Things Are Hard*. It sounds obvious, but in fact it's a great reminder that decisions with tough trade-offs don't come with an easy way out: trade-offs need to be acknowledged and faced. Helpful techniques exist for doing this and dealing with trade-offs often teaches us important stuff about ourselves and others. As author and activist Glennon Doyle says, "We can do hard things" (http://wecandohardthingspodcast.com).

In decisions made by adolescents, trade-offs can be a source of ambivalence, worry, excitement, and regret. In decisions made by groups of kids, trade-offs are often the source of disagreements because they tap directly into people's values – and that can get personal. Two students might agree that sneaking out after curfew to hang with a group of friends would be fun. One of them values his friends over his parents' rules, so he sneaks out. The other values his parents' goodwill more than time with friends, so he chooses to stay in. Different judgments are being made about the relative importance of the values affected by the choice.

One kid might try to convince another that the trade-offs he makes are more sensible than theirs. That's fine: respectful persuasion is basic to human nature. But ultimately there is no answer to someone who says, "Okay, I understand that's how you feel, and I feel differently." Or more formally, "I'm placing more importance than you are on some of the potentially affected values."

Trade-offs as part of collaborative decisions can be hard for kids to talk about because of these interpersonal differences. It can even be hard to have a good discussion about trade-offs with ourselves. Why? Because most of us choose to focus on the upside of a choice and avoid or minimize downsides. A recent graduate could be excited about their new job and focus on the extra pay, but not want to admit or even think much about the one hour of extra commuting added to their life each weekday. Trade-offs bring up specific elements of choices and force adolescents to move from grand concepts or abstractions to something very real. As a decision mentor you can help to bring this message home by highlighting the reality of trade-offs. Once a decision is made and implemented, the hypothetical can become real.

Hidden Influences on Our Choices

In the authors' roles as teachers and researchers, their hope is that learning the skills of effective decision making will translate into a better quality of life for teenagers (and for their decision mentors, of course). But we'd be naïve to not recognize that some of these same lessons are secretly being used by companies around the world with the more self-serving goal of increasing their sales and bottom-line profits.

Hidden influences on how teenagers make trade-offs provide a good example. One of the more common manipulations is known as the **decoy effect**, a cunning pricing strategy that encourages someone to switch from a cheaper to a more expensive option. Suppose both of the twin kids in your life, out with friends at the mall, are looking to buy a set of headphones. The store they visit displays two options: the cheaper set has decent frequency response, low total harmonic distortion (THD) and moderate impedance (60 Ohms) whereas the other, more expensive headphones have a wider frequency response (especially at the high end, creating a "brighter" sound), less THD, and higher impedance (over 300 Ohms). It's a tough choice, so they turn for help to a friendly salesperson. They tell the twins not to worry, that there is a third option: it's only a little less expensive than the higher-end headphones but it offers a much better frequency range and far less THD than the cheaper pair. Then they subtly throw in a reminder that the price difference between the newly introduced intermediate headphones and the most expensive set really isn't that much money.

What is now going on in the heads of your twins? They have just been exposed to the decoy effect, which is designed to nudge consumers away from the lower-priced competitor and to shift their preferences to the more expensive target option (geez … for just a little more money I can get all those cool extra features …). It's a carefully studied effect (see Huber, Payne, & Puto, 1982): marketers of a product will purposely increase choice complexity (e.g., presenting three options rather than two) to create confusion and anxiety and steer the teenage consumer in a particular direction – all in the name of being helpful! Happily, knowing about the decoy effect can also arm young consumers against it and avoid the hindsight regret that comes with paying more than intended.

A common source of difficulty for young decision makers is facing up to trade-offs when balancing short-term versus long-term considerations. Of course, words like *short-term* or *long-term* will vary among contexts: *short* might be a few minutes, hours, or weeks; *long* might be a few days, months, or years. But the behaviour is common, with many young decision makers falling into the well-known decision trap of ***myopia*** – placing too much importance on the short-term consequences of a choice and failing to consider longer-term effects.

The solution to recurrent myopia, as with many other aspects of good decision making, is twofold. First, help the young person you're working with recognize the importance of trade-offs over time. Bring up examples of attractive short-term options in your own life that you declined to follow only after consideration of their longer-term effects. Personal stories are a great help here, and if the stories are about yourself then there will be a level of safety and comfort (and perhaps even humour!) for the kid who is listening. Second, help the youth to activate their own thinking about the time dimension of consequences as a regular event, so they will consistently and quickly start to ask themselves questions about the longer-term outcomes that might follow from their choices.

Balancing Competing Values

Making trade-offs requires that kids make use of their fast *and* slow thinking systems – both their intuitive way to make sense of the world and their more analytical reasoning skills. The quality of trade-off decisions often comes down to how well these two systems get along and communicate with each other, which requires attention and some knowledge of the ways in which the faster parts of the brain can undermine the quality of decision making.

One aspect of trade-off decisions that messes with slower thinking is that the outcomes of a choice can be wide-ranging, which means it becomes harder to balance or compare them (yet another reason why a simple "pros and cons" list is not enough). We all face this dilemma when making choices involving spending money on clothing that's not really needed versus making a loan payment. A comparison between these two options taps into the very different nature of the values, and in these situations the faster System 1 often steps up, pushes aside the slower System 2, and directs attention to the most prominent values or the more immediate outcomes. And remember, trade-off decisions are especially tough for young people because the frontal cortex of an adolescent's brain – where the multisided consequences of a pending decision are sorted out – is still developing.

Consider actions to reduce adverse effects of climate change. A young person can recognize that the long-term consequences of climate change may well be catastrophic and have a firm commitment to do what they can to address it. Yet in their day-to-day decisions the more visceral near-term considerations, such as comfort or convenience, tend to win out. Despite the best of intentions, nothing much changes because they like their old pick-up truck, air conditioner, and fresh vegetables flown in from South America all winter. In general, the emotional attraction of near-term considerations is more prominent in trade-offs than the hard-to-visualize and less tangible long-term impacts of their decision.

This ongoing battle between fast and slow thinking also means choices are highly susceptible to what would seem to be minor, and presumably irrelevant, variations in how trade-off questions are posed – the "framing of consequences" issue that we first raised in the previous chapter. How trade-off information is presented can dramatically affect the relative importance decision makers place on the different values. Because making trade-offs always involves a balancing across values, the ones in the spotlight get more emotional attention.

Descriptions of Trade-offs Make a Difference

Here's a classic example of how trade-offs can vary depending on how a decision is framed. We might assume that doctors selecting treatments for seriously ill (and possibly terminal) patients use a very rational, thoughtful approach to making choices. But doctors are people, first and foremost, and prone to many of the same judgmental biases as anyone else. Working with physicians in one of the top hospitals in the US, researchers tested the doctors' recommendations for surgery versus radiation therapy under two decision frames. One described surgery outcomes in terms of survival rates, showing that the operation was successful 90 percent of the time: 9 times out of 10, the patient survived. The other frame described surgery outcomes in terms of mortality, showing that the operation was not successful 10 percent of the time: 1 time out of 10, the patient died. Despite the fact that the two descriptions are technically equivalent and despite the fact that physicians are supposed to be some of the savviest professionals when it comes to thinking about trade-offs, the recommendations they made to patients showed a significantly higher preference for surgery when results were reported using the frame emphasizing survival (McNeil et al., 1982).

This stronger emotional response to what's in the spotlight is universal. One way for mentors to help young decision makers deal with trade-offs is to encourage them to be proactive by thinking in advance about the choices that are likely to come up, when they have time to reflect and discuss issues with friends, family, and teachers. This proactive thinking reduces the spotlight effect and helps keep the slower and more effortful thinking system in the picture.

In our introductory section of this book, we described Ben Franklin's pros and cons approach to making tough decisions. While we agree he was a pretty smart guy, there is a lot he didn't know about making good decisions. In particular, lots of decision errors can arise when a simple pros and cons technique is used to make important trade-offs. Earlier in the book we didn't have a common language to describe these problems, but now we do – so here's our own short list of what's wrong with pros and cons, especially in the context of dealing with trade-offs.

- **Vague descriptions.** Your list might show a "high risk" of injury on the cons side (something to be avoided) or a "large possible financial gain" on the pros side. Sounds important, but what do these terms mean? How high a risk and for what types of injury? How large a gain and what does it mean that the gain is "possible" (is it very likely or very unlikely to occur?)? You don't know what you're balancing without precise descriptions of what is involved. Sometimes this is possible but often it isn't. The tendency is to proceed with the decision in spite of vague descriptions of potential consequences.

- **Double counting.** Suppose a pros list shows that a youth's parents could agree with a choice and their friends could also be happy with it. Is this one entry (e.g., people will be happy?) or is it sensible to count friends' reactions and parents' reactions as two separate entries? And what if some friends might not be pleased with the choice, are you now up to three entries? Is this just being specific or are you

158

counting the same thing multiple times? And are all the entries equally important or does quality (as well as quantity) also count? If some pros or cons are more important than others, then counting them all as having equal weight in a decision would be misleading.

- **Premature selection of options.** Your pros and cons list is always related to a specific decision you might make. But what if there are other, alternative choices that you've neglected or not paid attention to – will you decide to act after completing your pros and cons on only one option or will you also look into other, perhaps far better alternatives? As emphasized in the chapter on decision framing (Move 1), you won't get the choice right if you are dealing with the wrong decision.

- **Incomplete list of consequences.** It's not easy to think of all the possible consequences of a decision, which means that pros and cons lists usually ignore important considerations. Franklin anticipates this by suggesting that he often takes a "day or two" for "further consideration," which is fine if you have all the time in the world before making your choice. But most of us – including most youth – want to make decisions more quickly, so we're likely to be working from incomplete lists of outcomes.

- **Timing and uncertainty of consequences.** Your pros and cons list probably includes some things that are expected to take place quite soon and other things that may not happen for a long time. It also probably includes some things that are certain to happen and other things that may or may not take place. There are good ways to incorporate timing and uncertainty into decisions, but it's not something easily done as part of quickly comparing and crossing out items on a list.

- **Neglect of process**. A pros and cons list focuses on the outcomes of a decision: the good and bad things expected to take place as a result of the choice. But decisions aren't only about outcomes, they are also about *process* – how things are done and who is involved versus simply what is likely to happen. A decision may be of low quality because some people are left out, or because it takes too long to realize the benefits, or because other people's feelings end up being hurt along the way. Process matters.

The bottom line is that trade-offs inevitably involve finding a balance between pros and cons – benefits and costs, good things and bad, gains and losses – but coming up with simple lists is only a starting point. Pros-and-cons methods do not take advantage of all we've learned since the time of Franklin about how the brain processes information and the nature of gains and losses.

Balancing Gains and Losses

Jo was excited. A kid at school had agreed to sell them his skateboard. Jo checked it out on the weekend and it was exactly the skateboard they wanted. Unfortunately, a couple of days after scheduling a meet up, the seller messaged them with bad news: he had sold the board to someone else for a higher price. Jo was upset but there was nothing they could do about it. The board they wanted was gone. The next day Jo told a friend about the ordeal.

"My brother has that exact same board and never uses it," said the friend. "I'll bet he'd be happy to sell it to you for the same price."

Despite getting the identical board a few days later, Jo didn't feel like it had worked out – somehow, the loss of the original board felt bigger than the gain of the new board.

What's going on for Jo? Turns out the extra emotion around the loss is perfectly normal. Research shows that human beings feel losses more strongly than they do gains: the gain of a new identical board does not offset the loss of the original board. Kahneman and Tversky (1979), two of the field's top researchers, explain it in terms of everyone having a built-in understanding of how changes in their values refer back to a starting point, an initial level of satisfaction. Gains and losses are assessed in reference to that starting point, with gains counting for only about one-half as much as losses. The bottom line? Losses "loom larger" than gains. It's not a bias, nor is it something to be overcome through good decision making. It's simply how human beings are hard-wired.

The phenomenon of losses being felt more strongly than equal gains is powerful and widespread. Yet its effect is often underappreciated. Whether a change is viewed as a loss or gain is often the result of an unconscious choice of decision frame. If someone is thinking about starting a fitness program after a long period of being inactive, they could think about it in terms of making gains (and becoming more fit) or reclaiming something that has been lost (returning to a former fitness level). The same choice of frame faces government officials seeking to clean up pollution: a river can be made cleaner (thinking of it as a gain) or it can be brought back to its former glory (thereby restoring what has been lost over time). The choice of a frame, whether intentional or not, recasts the associated trade-offs and can contribute strongly to which choice is made.

The Value of Belonging

Canadian economist Jack Knetsch tested the idea that we value things in our possession more than identical replacements (Knetsch, 1989). Identical coffee mugs were passed out to two groups of young adults (college students). A few minutes later – hardly long enough to form an attachment – one group was asked how much they would pay to purchase their mug, the other was asked their selling price. To Jack's surprise, the average *selling* price responses were consistently 2 to 3 times higher than the average *purchase* price. Numerous other experiments confirmed this same trait, referred to as the **endowment effect**: the mere fact that something is viewed as part of our endowment and thus seen to belong to us (a coffee cup, membership in a group, a shared belief) significantly increases our perception of its worth.

Okay – take a deep breath and make the leap from coffee mugs to political movements. One of the leading explanations for the polarization of our current society is that people are giving less attention to the truth of information and instead care far more about their own sense of belonging to a group or a point of view. The good feelings that arise from this sense of belonging – particularly in a world where many people tend to feel alone and unseen – outweigh any other concerns. Just as with the seemingly irrational extra value attached to a coffee mug that is *mine*, there can be a large extra value attached to belonging to a group that is *mine* because the people in it supposedly accept me and share my views. For school-aged kids, belonging to a group may be so important that they radically adjust how they dress or talk. Similarly, they might pretend to like a certain type of music or sport just to fit into the norms of a group.

Making Collaborative Trade-offs

Most trade-off decisions take place in collaboration with other people. This makes things both easier (all those great new inputs!) and harder (all those annoying new inputs!), depending on the mix of personalities and values among the decision-making group. Good collaborative choices emerge when participants know their own values, listen to what others have to say, and are open-minded when it comes to negotiating a final decision. We highlight three considerations:

- Can the choice be simplified?
- What if the dialogue is on social media?
- Do participants care about reaching consensus?

Simplify

Remember the concert ticket consequence table from Move 4? It's shown again below to illustrate how the friends involved could choose to simplify their choice by eliminating one or more of the options by making trade-offs. Look at the view and comfort rows: Options B and C are identical. In terms of arrival time (60 minutes before the start vs. 75 minutes) Option B dominates. That just leaves the cost, and here too Option B (because it's lower in cost) is preferred over C. Since C has no advantages over B, why keep it in the mix?

This leaves our concert goers with a simpler decision between Options A and B only. Option A has a better view but it's much more expensive and our friends would need to arrive a half-hour earlier. On balance, is the better view worth it? That's the trade-off this decision turns on.

Values	Option A: in front of stage	Option B: bleachers	Option C: middle
View	Excellent	Good	Good
Cost	$$$$	$	$$
Comfort	Fair	Fair	Fair
Arrival time	90 minutes	60 minutes	75 minutes

Many of the trade-offs involved in collaborative decisions are not as clear cut as in our concert ticket example because they require identifying and balancing concerns that are harder to define and measure than the cost of a ticket or the quality of views. For example, choices might bring up difficult emotions or tap into past experiences and memories. Defining these as part of a consequence table can be done, but it's less straightforward.

The dynamics of a family or classroom allow for decision mentors to design decision-making opportunities for youth to deal with content (family choices or curriculum topics) while also learning the process of thoughtful, open-minded decision making. You might want to try making a decision *with* the youth you mentor, moving through the Decision-Maker Moves together. School provides lots of opportunities for students to make collaborative decisions and to polish their negotiating and listening skills. From classroom projects to student governments, the collaborative decisions youth face in groups require them to draw on a rich skill set that includes thinking critically about their own values and trade-offs, considering multiple perspectives on an issue, determining facts from fictions, and engaging in shared problem solving.

Sixty-five students in grades 6 to 8 at Q'shintul/Mill Bay Nature School streamed into one end of the gym with the comfort of a well-practised weekly routine. After the students found their seats, the first speaker was called to address their peers and teachers – as equal members of their learning community – to present a decision opportunity they wanted to bring to the group.

The young speaker posed her question about upcoming school Halloween celebrations: "Are we okay with scary costumes?" Many children quickly shouted out their support for scary costumes.

Kim, the Head Learner (aka the school principal), spoke up to make space for other ideas. "Even though there are a lot of people who like scary costumes, we need to hear from some other perspectives."

In response, a teacher shared: "When I was a little girl, I had violence in my home. So when I saw scary costumes at Halloween it would maybe scare me a little more. So now that I'm an adult, I feel worried – which is kinda an adult way of feeling scared – that for some of our kids who maybe come from families that aren't as peaceful or who have experienced violence in their homes a scary costume could really make them sad or turn school into a scary place to be."

An older student then shared his story: "I was really scared when I was four because I went to a haunted house ... and it scared me so bad that I'm really scared of those costumes now." The room was quiet as those who had been shouting their assent were now considering the experiences of their peers.

Kim took the mic and shared her thoughts. "For me, school is for learning and growing. When our brains are afraid, they stop learning. Your parents send you to school to learn and grow – I come here to create a space for people to learn and grow. And when people are scared, they can't learn and grow."

Other perspectives were shared, and there was a discussion of the difference between violent and scary. Kim kept track of the thinking and concerns. Ultimately, the students agreed to hold further discussions in their classes around the differences that had surfaced and the trade-offs they had heard.

Kim commented that it's amazing "what kids can do when you open a space for them to do it. To create this [space where adults and youth make decisions together] is messy. Perhaps it's the mess that scares many adults away from creating spaces like what we have here. But it's worth it."

Collaborative decisions, whether among adults or (as in this case) involving both students and teachers, are frequently messy. The adults must listen closely for themes as they emerge while emphasizing and being true to the community's values and identity. As Head Learner Kim describes it, "When we hold these values at the heart of our decisions, we can trust that our choices will be the right decisions – or at least as right as they can be in any one moment."

Digital Dialogue

The nature of shared decision making has changed now that digital dialogues are so pervasive. With digital interactions, large numbers of people from different locations and time zones can work together to address tough choices. That's a plus, but it's also easy for participants to hide behind screens of anonymity. Without a physical presence, we lack the relationship cues provided by face-to-face communication and it can be more difficult to trust each other or move to shared decisions.

We are big believers in the benefits of digital sharing and storytelling. But these focused, task-centred dialogues are different from the quick, distracted back-and-forth that often takes place on social media platforms. These spaces tend to invite automatic and fast-thinking-based emotional responses that create unintended communication of inaccurate information or intentional communication of disinformation. It is easy to manipulate rather than inform on these platforms.

Research has also shown that social media exchanges tend to demonstrate less concern about the feelings and reactions of other people. Studies show that the richness and openness of a values-based dialogue is often compromised and, because clarification is not always possible, the person on the receiving end of a message can easily be left confused, frustrated, or outraged – without the other parties in the dialogue necessarily even being aware of this reaction. This dynamic can result in more extreme interactions, even with text messaging. This is a problem decision mentors can highlight.

Wrangling Consensus

Consensus is a fine idea and goal, but it is not always possible because a group's young decision makers may hold different values and want different outcomes. Good news! Consensus is not needed; with a willingness to negotiate and be open-minded, members of the group can still agree to support an action even when their levels of enthusiasm for it, or their reasons for accepting it, are different. What is required is to clear blockages out of the way, so that the heated disagreements that can accompany trade-offs aren't allowed to stop the decision-making process. These blockages can arise from a wide range of sources:

- **Relationships.** Jacquie might not trust or even like Monica, so she will resist any of Monica's ideas rather than being open-minded about what she says. Can Jacquie learn to unhook the ideas from the messenger?

- **Language.** Sal might be equating one of their values – fun – with outdoor activities while Mia might be using fun to describe more quiet, largely indoor activities. So they express the same value but have different options in mind. Decision mentors can help by asking for clarity and more precise understandings of words.

- **Dialogue.** The group might simply have trouble listening to one another, for example they may be engaging in the rules of debate (trying to convince the other side of their own perspective) rather than the rules of open dialogue, so it makes it more difficult to learn and adjust.

- **Poor options.** If none of the options on the table are appealing, it's time to stop, have a brainstorming session, and get more creative by questioning constraints and old habits. A good starting point is to consider staying with the "default" or "status quo" option; if everyone is unhappy with keeping things as they are, this can supply a push to come up with new options that, even if less than great, will better reflect the group's expressed trade-offs.

Here's a specific strategy to overcome a blocked discussion: ask the members of a class or group to take a temperature check by weighing in on an option. They can do this by stating whether they Endorse it, Accept it, or Oppose it. Those who somewhat grudgingly accept a decision (along with those who enthusiastically endorse it) are supportive of it, even if they would prefer a different option. Often a discussion can reveal changes to an option that will shift some Oppose votes over to Accept votes.

It was the first week of school and Joanne Calder wanted to introduce her grade 6 and 7 students to the Decision-Maker Moves as a way to help them take the lead on a seating plan. Using visual aids from a Decision-Maker Tool called Guts vs. Heads (download it at www.deltalearns.ca/decisions), she guided the class through a structured dialogue until they hit an impasse: two students outright opposed all of the options.

Just at the point when Joanne started to worry that this experiment had failed, one of her students turned to the boys in frustration and asked them, "What will it take for you to agree to one of these options?!"

Turns out, they simply wanted to be allowed to sit next to one another for the first few weeks, so the students tweaked one of the options to include this arrangement. Problem solved and everybody happy, most of all the relieved teacher. The question her student asked is a brilliant one – what will it take?

Trade-offs Involving Risk

The trade-offs made in Joanne's class involved no risk, only preferences. This made it a relatively simple decision. Risk introduces new dynamics for you to understand as a decision mentor so you can assist young decision makers to think through their values and the options in a way that fits with their personality as well as your bottom-line concern for their safety. No kid wants their parent or other influential adult to keep yelling "Be careful, be careful" every time they head out the door, and no adult wants to see a kid be injured. You will know many of these distinctions intuitively, so we will touch on them briefly below to bring them into your conscious awareness.

Differences in Risk Understanding

Youth typically have a different sense of risk than adults. They are more tolerant of some risks and less tolerant of others than the adults in their lives. Many younger people are willing to try activities that might be viewed by their elders as better left alone, or at least postponed until a later age. Some of these activities are subject to rules imposed by adults in an effort to control behaviour: most jurisdictions set a minimum legal age on drinking alcohol or driving a car; other activities (involving narcotics, for example) are subject to outright bans. The reasoning in such cases typically has to do, at least in part, with the acknowledgment of trade-offs across risks that require a level of informed understanding and an ability to control impulsive behaviours.

These age-related differences in risk tolerance can result in additional stress (think of parents worrying about the activities they fear their kids are involved in) or in additional injuries and even deaths for youth (think of out-of-bounds snowboarders or experimentation with drugs). And new risks appear with disarming regularity. During the global COVID-19 pandemic, for example, several new risks were added to every kid's list: suddenly keeping a two-meter distance from friends and obeying proper social distancing were viewed as essential responses to a new source of risk-based trade-offs. Kids responded in ways that reflected their values and worldviews. Individuals with a very low tolerance for risks often refused to leave their homes without masks and gloves. In more extreme cases, some refused to attend mandatory classes or washed all their clothes as soon as they returned from the grocery. Other kids, however, went about their lives as if nothing much was awry, no masks or distancing; either they trusted different information or their tolerance to COVID-19 risks was higher.

There is another side to this story: the available information about risks may not be interpreted accurately, either because it is intentionally presented in a way designed to misinform or because a choice exceeds the decision-making capabilities of the youth. As noted by Baruch Fischhoff (2008) – a risk researcher interested in the decisions of adolescents – youth need the right amount of risk at the right times so they can exercise their independence in a safe way. The message is clear: adults in the picture will need to make tough decisions about when to step in to provide a helpful perspective and when to stand back, trusting the intelligence and skills of the young decision maker.

Differences in Risk Perceptions

How a person perceives risks is partially related to the available facts but also reflects their psychological and emotional response. Differences in risk perceptions across adolescents help to explain why the same person who is highly tolerant of risks from COVID-19 might be deathly afraid when it comes to flying in an airplane.

Consider the risks of driving a car compared to the risk of an earthquake. The scientific information may show that a youth's chance of getting seriously injured or killed while driving is much higher than their likelihood of injury or death due to an earthquake. But for many people the earthquake risk is perceived to be far larger, because exposure is largely out of their control and involuntary – driving risks are familiar and to a large degree assumed to be within our control. Same thing with shark attacks versus losing your footing on a stairway. Far more people are killed each year due to falls within their homes than by sharks, but few horror films place a flight of stairs in the starring role.

The big question for you and the kids in your life is whether their risk tolerances are both informed and serving their best interests. Stories about higher-risk-taking kids are well known. But to what extent, and in what ways, are higher risk tolerances serving their interests? In the short run, perhaps they are. But will this same risk-loving perspective remain helpful in the long run? These are questions for the decision mentor to discuss with a young decision maker; it's not necessary (nor is it likely) that both the adult and the youth will agree on all risk-related choices, but that doesn't mean you shouldn't have the conversation.

What If the Decision Mentors Don't Agree?

We've been assuming all along that there is one decision mentor who is working with either one younger individual (e.g., a parent or coach) or a group of kids (e.g., a teacher). But there might be multiple mentors: two or more parents and step-parents, two or more teachers or coaches. What if these mentors are giving the kid different advice, perhaps because they have different perspectives on the world and on what matters? For example, one mentor could be looking at a teen's summer job option as being a perfect match with their personality and future goals, whereas another mentor could be actively discouraging the youth from going to the job interview because they don't see it as a good fit. What's a twelve- or fifteen-year-old to do in such a situation?

Each decision context is unique, so there is no one answer. However, it helps to think of this dilemma as a choice (whose advice do I run with?) within a choice (should I apply for the job?). And it helps to remember the Decision-Maker Moves: if there is conflicting advice from two mentors, which one has explicit or implicit values most closely aligned with those of the younger decision maker? What outcomes are likely if the advice of one mentor or the other is followed? And perhaps both mentors have only a partial understanding of the decision, which means that the kid may select a third option because they frame the choice differently.

What's the bottom line on trade-offs involving risks? The key for a decision mentor is to avoid blanket judgments about a young person's risk tolerance and realize that (a) risk tolerances tend to shift as we age, generally toward the more cautious side of things, and (b) taking on risks that seem crazy to one person could be highly beneficial and work out well for another. As long as a young decision maker's choices are in line with who they are and make sense in the larger context, and as long as there are open lines of communication between the decision mentor and the decision maker, then encouraging autonomy that matches a decision maker's competence and risk tolerances is generally okay.

Time to Choose

Once trade-offs have been recognized, defined, and considered, your young decision maker is ready to make their choice. If they are quite confident they have the information needed to make the decision, there is no reason to wait any longer – choose!

When the consequences of the decision are not all that important (whether to stay home or go over to a friend's house on Friday night) then the choice presumably will be made quickly. If it's of greater significance (purchasing a car or computer) then the choice probably involves coordinating with others and may take longer. Either way, it's generally a source of relief when the choice has been made and it's time to move on. But not always, because no matter how diligent the preparation and no matter how closely the Decision-Maker Moves have been followed, the need to make a choice sometimes gives rise to new emotional responses or even new concerns that can add a challenging dose of human reality to the decision process.

> One of the authors (Robin) moved to a new city with his wife and young child when he was in his mid-thirties. Houses were not so expensive at that time so after making sure their jobs would work out the house search began. This was to be their first house purchase; after clarifying their objectives and mortgage possibilities and after looking around for a couple of weeks, Robin and his wife were relieved to find a great house – within walking distance of both their jobs, near to schools and stores, priced fairly, and in a neighbourhood with lots of diversity (people from different countries and a variety of housing types and prices). They quickly put in a bid and it was accepted, followed by handshakes and hugs all around (and a small deposit of course). End of story, right? But no ... That night the much younger Robin began to worry: could he and his partner really afford to buy a house? What if something went wrong and a new roof or furnace was needed? What if ... Following a few days of self-torture Robin and his wife sat down again with the sellers and,

with massive apologies, explained that they had "got cold feet" and would have to withdraw their offer. After some unpleasant negotiating it was agreed: the house would be put back on sale.

Two days later both Robin and his wife started to regret their decision, feeling that they had let anxiety and inexperience triumph over the logic favouring such a large first-ever purchase. After speaking with friends and a reassuring talk with an amused bank manager, they returned once again to the bewildered sellers and said, "Guess what? We want to rebuy the house we already bought and then walked away from!"

Demonstrating patience and good heartedness, the sellers (for the second time) agreed to sell the house and, this time, everything went through as planned. Robin and his wife and kids lived happily in the house for many years, comfortable in the knowledge they had, at least eventually, made a good decision. And Robin learned something valuable about the role of emotions and nonrational thinking in decision making, which helped to shape his professional career over the next several decades.

The act of choosing, no matter how much information or experience you have, can be challenging. Depending on the nature of the consequences and what is asked of the young decision maker, it can be difficult to separate out the pull of emotions from a more reflective decision-making perspective. And depending on the significance of the decision, making a choice can call for courage and optimism in addition to knowledge of relevant values and facts.

Is There a Role for Artificial Intelligence?

One of many topics beyond the scope of this book is artificial intelligence (AI) and its role, now and in the future, in the decision-making practices of adolescents. It is widely acknowledged that AI input can prove both helpful and troublesome, as has been shown by recent experiences with generative AI applications such as ChatGPT or Midjourney. Although we share many of the concerns raised about AI, in some circumstances a strong case can be made for involving robots or other AI-powered helpers to assist people in assembling the information needed to make a decision. One of the obvious advantages of AI is that it would be better than most people at resisting the emotional pull of manipulative stories and engaging in statistical reasoning. AI tools also can take into consideration a larger number of factors than the human brain; already AI helps police decipher fingerprints, doctors read x-rays, and pharmaceutical companies develop new drugs because it can very quickly process large amounts of information. Yet it's essential to remember that people still need to sift through any AI output to test its relevance and quality and, in many cases, to determine whether the information is likely to be useful or significant in the context of a particular decision.

All the nonrational factors that openly or covertly influence our choices can play an even larger role in decisions made by young people, who by virtue of their age face many first-time (and therefore unfamiliar) choices. Perhaps the consequences of the choice are uncertain, with high costs associated with things not working out. Perhaps the choice is controversial, holding some potential to burn bridges with friends. In such cases it's natural and even healthy that a decision – often both before and after the choice is made – keeps getting re-evaluated and turned over from the perspective of "what if I'd chosen differently, would things have turned out better or worse?" And the list of reasons for self-doubt in making a choice goes on. Perhaps the choice is irreversible (the tattoo you thought would be so terrific) and you have regret as the misgivings set in. Or perhaps you learn more information, but it's too late to adjust your trade-offs: the computer purchased last week at what seemed to be a good price has just gone on sale at a lower price.

In all these cases (and many more) the young decision maker may repeatedly question whether they've done the right thing. As the decision mentor, you can provide a calming voice, reassuring them that some measure of self-questioning is entirely natural and even healthy – making a choice can sometimes feel a bit too much like jumping off a cliff. Perhaps tell a story or two about when you were younger and found yourself in the same place. Often the decision-making cliff becomes a little less steep because it's possible to make adjustments over time or to learn things from one decision that help with future similar decisions. These adjustments are the subject of the final Decision-Maker Move.

Weigh Trade-offs: For Your Back Pocket

- Trade-offs are difficult. They can't be avoided and when young decision makers ignore trade-offs they often end up facing surprising and unwelcome consequences.
- Encourage a young decision maker to be as clear as possible about what is to be gained or lost through a decision. Try to avoid vague phrases (for example, terms such as high or low: high or low compared to what?). The lack of clarity can mislead an individual's decisions and result in miscommunication in collaborative decisions,

because people interpret words differently. Talking helps, especially when risks are involved.

- When thinking about trade-offs, help the young decision maker keep their focus on the choice at hand and not get pulled into side discussions about personalities or irrelevant information. Decision mentors help kids organize their thoughts and feelings around what matters for their choice.

- Both you and the youth you're helping need to pay attention to your intuitive, emotional responses to a pending trade-off as well as your more analytical, reasoned responses. Check in with the decision maker to discover what is driving their first reaction: is it based in reality and in line with their own values or does it come from someone or something outside of themselves?

Decision Traps

Myopia: the widespread tendency to overemphasize short-term considerations to the neglect of longer-term considerations. This tendency is especially strong in young decision makers, for whom the longer-run may be anything that could occur after today.

Trade-off avoidance: because facing trade-offs can be difficult a common way to deal with the challenge of trade-offs is to pretend they don't exist or will magically disappear. They do and they won't.

Practice

For Parents

Play "Would you rather." This can be a fun game – expressing preferred choices between options – to play when travelling or waiting in line or whenever you have a few open minutes with a teenager. No matter what choices you come up with in this game, be sure to ask *Why?* after each answer. This exploration of *why* creates an opportunity to practise thinking about consequences and trade-offs. Warning though: it might cause some eye rolling so choose your questions wisely. Here are some ideas: *Would you rather ...* Eat a bucket of blueberries or a bucket of popcorn? Be a scientist or an artist? Go on an expedition to the Arctic or spend a week in a submarine?

Watch TV quiz shows. Participants are constantly put in the position of needing to decide if they want to keep the modest prizes already won or go for something bigger and grander at the risk of losing what they've already gained. Depending on how the conversation goes, you can see the emphasis that's placed on either the potential gains or the potential losses that will accompany their choice.

For Those Who Work with Kids

- **Play it out.** This can be done verbally. Basically, walk the decision maker through what happens if … For a social worker it might sound like this: "Okay, so you want to go live with your dad. What does that mean for your social life? What does that mean for your relationship with your dad? What responsibilities would you have at your dad's?"

- **Sketch a *decision tree*.** A decision tree is a diagram that, depending on your answer to a question, will take you down one path or another to the next question and so on and so on until you get to an answer. If you are a teacher, build thinking about consequences into your lesson planning. You might consider a decision that a world figure or local official made that is relevant to your curriculum. In groups, have students research how various groups are responding to the decision. For example, a decision about building a new bridge will be met with responses from commuters, environmentalists, the townspeople who live near the proposed site, transit enthusiasts, and taxpayers. A decision about a change in driver licensing will be met with responses from parent groups, youth, lawyers, police agencies, insurance companies, and government. In either scenario, these groups would identify trade-offs critical to the decision or to aspects of the decision. This is also a great way to engage learners in understanding diverse perspectives without taking things personally or having much at stake.

- **Teach dialogue skills instead of or alongside debate skills.** There is much to be learned from cultures where listening and engaging with living beings (human and nonhuman) in conversation is the default. When we engage in dialogue we engage in a relationship of reciprocity. In relationships like this we can see how diversity offers us a strong way forward and why the polarization that often comes from debate contributes to an unsustainable future.

Go Deeper

- *Risk* by Baruch Fischhoff and John Kadvany (Oxford University Press, 2011). This "very short introduction" to risk provides a comprehensive, and highly readable, overview of the field and illustrates key points with examples drawn from the authors' extensive research and experiences.

- *A Promised Land* (Viking, 2020). This memoir by former US President Barack Obama presents stories from his life and early years as President that provide a glimpse into how he (and colleagues) addressed a series of tough trade-offs associated with health care, income sharing, and other national policies. Whether or not you agree with Obama's perspective, the book provides a fascinating look into how significant choices and difficult trade-offs at the national and international level are made.

- The blockbuster 1997 movie *Titanic* (dir. James Cameron) is full of choices involving trade-offs, from the initial decision to build such a massive ocean liner to the decision to take the northern route to all the choices made by Rose, Jack, and the other lead characters as to how they would spend their time while on the ship and, of course, how they would try to save themselves once it became clear the vessel was going to sink. *Titanic* is considered one of the great movies of all time because it combines romance and tragedy – and lying behind every romance and every tragedy are a host of decisions, some of which in hindsight might well be questioned.

6

· · · · ·

Move 6: Stay Curious and Adjust

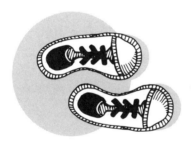

The Skidegate dialect of the Haida, an Indigenous Nation on the West Coast of Canada, has a phrase for "staying curious." *Gina gii Giixan aanagung* means "to look around with curiosity and intent." This Haida concept holds more than curiosity; it conveys the idea of staying observant with the world *on purpose*. It suggests an active stance. Staying curious by asking questions, paying attention, and learning new things takes energy and action.

The *Stay Curious and Adjust* Decision-Maker Move is about decision makers being in a learning relationship with their choices, actively seeking to uncover and learn from new information based on their own lives and experiences as well as the conversations they have with others. It's a recognition that many choices are repeated (with minor changes), so there are ample opportunities for self-learning and making adjustments. And few choices are truly standalone and permanent, both because the context for decisions changes over time and because a person's values also change – consider the change in a thirteen-year-old's values as compared to when they are nineteen.

Staying curious implies an active monitoring of our choices, staying alert to our own and others' decisions and how they might be adjusted and improved over time.

Staying curious implies iteration: we decide to do something but then revisit that choice in light of what we've later learned, either about ourselves or about the consequences of our actions. This re-examination might lead to a shift in the preferred option, or perhaps a change in the scale or timing of something that's being done.

Clara has two teenagers who for various reasons "went off the rails."

"They stopped going to school, started doing drugs and one of them was constantly in trouble with the police. I was in a madhouse. I kept wondering what happened to my sweet children. But then I remembered – they are still here. I just have to believe in them, point them to their highest and best selves, and hold on."

There were a rough few years. Hospital visits, psych wards, drug issues, and occasionally avoidance of school were the norm in Clara's house. Now, looking back, Clara recalls how curiosity kept them all going. Her belief that the trajectory her children had chosen was temporary made space for dialogue and curiosity, even when her children saw little need for communication themselves.

Clara reflects, "Most of our world, much of our school system, teaches us to see things in black and white. But staying curious means staying open to what matters and reminding them of that – seeing possibility even after a path is chosen. It's about small steps often, not one step made permanent. The small steps all add up. So I kept pointing my kids to their values, their stories, their dreams. Even when they didn't see it. That's my job as their mom. To keep the window of possibility open. They'll make mistakes. And so few of those mistakes are permanent, definitive mistakes."

As it turns out, Clara's school district offered all sorts of alternative learning options and, in order to become aware of them and even create their own solution, her kids needed Clara to stay curious and keep "seeing the grey." So she guided them by linking information about the available schooling options back to their expressed values. And, in time, they saw more possibility as well. Her son eventually agreed to give one of the alternative programs a try. Clara reports, "He's thriving. Right now he is consistently going to school and doing well."

Clara is optimistic about her daughter's path as well but she is also realistic, so Clara added, "I'll remain consistently curious, checking in with both kids about how they're doing and how it all lines up with what they're thinking and what matters to them. We'll all adjust if we need to."

Flexibility is key to the long-term success of any decision-making strategy. Flexibility means staying current with the decision context and with who the decision maker is, especially given that adolescence is a period of constant growth and huge changes. As a decision mentor you can help youth avoid getting hooked by familiar habits that perhaps are better left behind or the lure of past successes that may no longer apply because the context has changed. Here are three things to keep in mind when trying to help kids stay curious and make adjustments.

1. **Our modern world is subject to what feels like constant change.** Teaching youth to be curious and actively monitor the quality of their choices increases their ability to adjust to changing circumstances and to make good choices in the long run. If youth can stay attuned to feedback about the quality of their choices and curious about what happens in their lives, they will be in a position to make even better choices in the future.

2. **Young decision makers need to remain sceptical and curious** about the principles or procedures they've developed to help with time-sensitive decisions. As youth age into reflective young adults, the situations they encounter will change and the principles appropriate at one time may not be any longer. Necessary revisions can come from self-reflection and by opening up new conversations with peers or family or teachers.

3. **Going forward with a tough decision requires courage and self-confidence.** Having a clear sense of what they want can increase a young person's sense of determination and confidence. Think about an eleven-year-old deciding about changing schools, or a thirteen-year-old wondering if they should come out at school, or a sixteen-year-old whose preferred career path is beginning to look very different from that envisioned by their parents. Well-timed support from a decision mentor can provide a critical boost of courage and confidence.

Feedback, Learning, and Iteration

The Decision-Maker Moves help people actively practise the art of inquiry – staying curious about others, about themselves, and about the world in which they live. A person who differs from you might well have an equally strong basis for believing what they do but their values are different. The tools provided by the Decision-Maker Moves encourage people to ask "Why is this important to you especially when it's not important to me" rather than jump to conclusions.

Values-focused exploration can change a confrontation into a conversation, hopefully overcoming misunderstanding and polarization.

The Decision-Maker Moves encourage young decision makers to seek information from parents, teachers, or friends and to think critically about this information. How reliable is the source? How accurate is it? Does it even really apply to this decision context? Asking these questions may lead to a shift in how the consequences of a decision are viewed. And it often means there is a need to slow down and collect new data. The process of constructing high-quality, long-term solutions and reaching agreement with others on their implementation may take some time.

The Perils of Premature Agreement

Particularly when we're making group decisions, back-and-forth conversations can become heated. Agreement may seem impossible. At this point fatigue can set in and the parties involved become less interested in inquiry and more interested in ending the conversation. At such times nearly any decision will do.

However, talking and thinking about the linkages between values, options, and consequences until a good decision can be made can build relationships. Be aware that one party in a decision will often push for a premature agreement because it's in their best interest, so they will use fatigue or bring in extraneous information as part of an intentional attempt to get the other(s) to agree to an outcome that's more in their own interest.

Emboldened by the Decision-Maker Moves, the bottom line is that we keep our ears and eyes, brains and hearts open and welcome alternative views. At best, practising curiosity and welcoming feedback will help us pay attention to a diversity of perspectives and enrich our lives through information and dialogue. And this learning – about the values and perspectives held by others and the different ways they interpret information about consequences – can change the stories youth create going forward.

The Power of Inquiry

Educators have known about the power of inquiry for decades now. Teachers from various parts of the world (Canada, the US, Wales, Spain, Sweden, Australia, New Zealand, England, Germany) use a model called the Spiral of Inquiry to help them collaborate to transform the quality and equity of learners' experiences (Halbert & Kaser, 2022). The Decision-Maker Moves are an important companion to the Spiral of Inquiry because an inquiry is essentially a series of linked decisions. Using the Decision-Maker Moves at key points as they move through the Spiral of Inquiry helps educators generate new and creative options while avoiding decision traps like confirmation bias and anchoring. This awareness deepens their thinking and can make the difference between spending a whole year learning about something that will truly impact student outcomes versus something that might feel good and be fun but have little transformative effect.

This willingness to pay attention to and (as needed) edit their own stories helps young decision makers overcome a trap known as the ***narrative fallacy***. This trap occurs whenever a decision maker gets hooked by the power or beauty of a story rather than the truth of the matter. Advertisers are masters at this, intentionally pulling young people into someone else's story that might well appear more attractive, at least at the moment, than does their own life – and all that's needed to grab your own little piece of paradise is a new pair of shoes, or a new tech device, or a short vacation. These stories we're told about things are so attractive that it's easy to lose sight of reality and stop asking critical questions (a good start: whose objectives are really being served by this story?).

Experience provides us all with opportunities for learning. It's no surprise that decisions made by young people – who presumably have less experience in many areas than the adults who live and work with them – can skip over things that later turn out to have been significant. And high-quality feedback unfortunately isn't always accessible. This was a problem in the early days of the COVID-19 pandemic: no one – including public health officials, scientists, and politicians – really knew what was going on because the virus was brand new. They could look to data on other viruses and earlier pandemics but they didn't know for sure how accurately their predictions would apply to COVID-19 behaviours.

Feedback is all about learning something new and then, if needed, making a shift in decisions to achieve a preferred result. Move 3 introduced the idea of ***sunk cost bias***, which leads to errors in our thinking that can encourage pursuing a course of action long after our more sensible side tells us it's no longer the right choice. Being open to feedback means you need to listen (for real) and that you have a sufficiently flexible course of action, one that retains the possibility of changing course and adapting.

The Gift of Mistakes

When a child comes to you and admits to making a mistake your first response is probably to be compassionate. This is someone you care about, after all, and something troubling has taken place in their life. Once you've moved on to talking about the issue, it helps to emphasize the point that mistakes are an unavoidable aspect of decision making and learning, part of everyone's experience in moving from a younger to an older person. Clearly some mistakes result in disasters (e.g., not filling your water containers before taking a hike through the desert) but others may result in learning that would be difficult to access any other way. Hence the dubious distinction made by Yogi Berra, baseball player and amateur philosopher, who is reported to have said about his team, "We made too many wrong mistakes."

What about when you observe that your teenage child, student or grandchild is about to undertake an action that may end up with undesirable consequences? Clearly your first obligation is to the safety of the teenager: you want to do what's needed to make sure their decision doesn't result in a negative life-changing event. But suppose the outcome you're worried about will end up resulting in a less severe consequence: embarrassment or inconvenience or one of those "in hindsight, I really wish I hadn't done that" moments (which all us adults have many of in our own memory bank!). Should you intervene or is it best to stand aside and let the teenager make their own choice and deal with the consequences? If an adult intervenes too often or prematurely the youth will be robbed of valuable learning opportunities. And because it narrows rather than enlarges the scope of their decision-making environment, the implied message is the opposite of trusting in or encouraging the agency and good sense of the younger person.

A good friend of Robin's tells the story of visiting an Indigenous wood carver who lives on the Pacific Coast, world-famous for the totem poles and other carvings he has made over several decades. On this particular day the man's teenage son was working alongside him, completing the rough carve-out on one portion of the 21-metre cedar pole. Robin's friend looked over and saw that the young man was holding onto the pole with one hand and carving in the direction of his fingers with what looked like a very sharp chisel. He became alarmed that an accident was about to happen and – interrupting the master carver to point out what was going on – said something along the lines of "I don't know if you've noticed, but your son looks like he is in danger of cutting off his finger." The older carver looked up briefly but then returned to his task. After a few moments he looked up at Robin's friend and said, "I've known a lot of four-fingered carvers, but I've never known a carver whose father told him what to do."

One of the main benefits of allowing and acknowledging mistakes that don't have disastrous consequences (a "good" vs. "bad" mistake?) is that mistakes provide feedback that passes on important information to a young decision maker. Assuming the mistakes remain small enough that nothing horrific occurs, then "good" mistakes can provide the raw material of learning – but only if there is clear feedback and the teenage decision maker is open, first to acknowledging that a mistake was made and second to doing something a little different next time around (and again being open to the new round of feedback). High-school dating experiences are a great example and should provide an inexhaustible source of humorous or horrifying stories for decision mentors to share with the kids they live or work with.

A common decision-making mistake, often referred to as the decision trap of **representativeness**, occurs when something new (maybe a person or an event) is too quickly slotted into the label or category used for what is already known. It's the opposite of inquiry or curiosity in action. Instead of being open and looking ahead to something novel and different, we refer back to what we think we already know. This decision trap often comes up in meeting new people. Because someone looks or talks or dresses like another person, we assume they will be like that other person. This trap is the basis for polarization and needs to be overcome for productive dialogue to take place. One of the best decision-making tools for overcoming the trap of representativeness is to bring more curiosity to the person or event in question; often the characteristics discovered through inquiry will reveal the misleading initial labelling. Consider this scenario.

Tanasha has always been interested in Artificial Intelligence (AI) and hopes to get a job at a small local start-up after graduating from her two-year computer programming course. With help from one of her teachers she arranges to meet the HR manager at a coffee shop downtown. She arrives promptly at 10 a.m. and sees two people sitting at the table by the window, one a well-dressed man in his thirties talking on the phone and the other a woman in her fifties dressed very simply. After he hangs up, Tanasha walks up to the table and extends her hand to the man – but it turns out that the woman is the CEO and the man her assistant. Tanasha makes a joke and hopes she can recover from her mistake.

Sometimes it can make sense to make intentional mistakes. Pharmaceutical companies do this when running trials with new drugs: instead of giving everyone the same dose, they try out three or four different doses of the new drug, often along with a blank or placebo, to test which is most effective. The company is sound in its decision-making logic that this approach is the best way to advance short-term learning, even though some people will receive better treatments than others.

In his last year of high school, Al enrolled in a work experience course that meant working in a field he was considering as an option for his post-secondary schooling: graphic design. One of his assignments is producing brochures about the houses offered for sale.

He knows his work will be inspected closely, by both the sellers and the prospective clients, so at first he focuses on displays using the template provided. The job goes okay and after a while Al starts to feel creative about it. For two consecutive open-house weekends he makes several slightly different versions of the brochures – one includes pictures that are a little larger with less text, one includes longer descriptions of the houses, another includes several pen-and-ink drawings Al created. He asks the real-estate agents to help keep track of what he's done and how clients respond.

By the end of the second weekend he has the results on the four different versions of the brochures (the original plus three new entrants) and he has learned some important things: one of the versions of the brochure didn't work (people couldn't make sense of it) and he did get a few complaints from people who received the initial version. But with the other two, Al found that his adjustments were able to move customers' satisfaction from "pretty darn good" to "amazing." He feels good about the outcome of his experiment and has learned something important. The next day, back at the office, he meets with his employers to see if he has their permission to take the same experimental approach into several other aspects of his job.

Admitting mistakes – both inadvertent and those you've planned for – can have one other benefit: it can make you appear more trustworthy to others. Research shows that people who recommend actions after admitting to a mistake tend to be more trusted than people who simply make a recommendation (Gallo, 2010). People are perceived as having gained experience and expertise that adds credibility to their opinion and later behaviour. We view this as a promising result, because if learning comes to be viewed as a positive asset rather than as evidence of poor judgment or a source of shame, perhaps it will be easier for people to stay curious, admit their mistakes, and try something new.

If we know there is a lot to learn about the likely consequences of a decision, it makes sense to stay flexible in our choices. This message is basic to success in most sports. If you are playing against an opposing team for the first time, you won't know as much as you'd like to about their strengths and weaknesses. You'll find out soon enough, of course, but you want to have a game plan that allows your team to stay flexible and incorporate changes in strategies based on the new learning. Often coaches will bring in plays that purposely test the ability of the opposing team to respond, looking for weaker players or spots they can exploit and stronger players or areas they will stay away from. The key for young decision makers is to realize that flexibility in your strategies, and the paired ability to revise options based on what is learned, is all the more helpful when you don't know some important things about the decision context.

Acknowledging Uncertainty

Uncertainty has come up repeatedly throughout this book, for good reason. Most youth, most of the time, tend to downplay the important role of uncertainty as part of the decision-making process. And in many cases uncertainty is simply ignored, a decision trap known as ***uncertainty neglect***. This trap is the false sense of short-term comfort that comes from setting uncertainty aside as if it were not in play. We all would like to have control over how the future will evolve, but the truth is that, in many important ways, we don't – so giving too little attention to uncertainty lowers a young decision maker's chances of accurately anticipating or responding to the outcomes of their choices.

This isn't always a bad thing. If everyone paused to consider all the more likely and less likely events that *could* occur once we decide to do something, then paralysis would set in and no one would ever actually do anything. Action and progress require that we carry on under the assumption that most highly likely things will happen and most highly unlikely things won't happen. And usually that's correct, so it's easy to feel confirmed in ignoring outcomes that are highly uncertain. But as the significance of the consequences grows – as we shift from a trip to the grocery for milk to choosing a trade school or a college to building a home in a floodplain to constructing a nuclear power station – it makes more and more sense to pay attention to the uncertainty connected to very unlikely but highly consequential events.

The Laws of Probability

Probabilities are often treated as if they were mysterious, a concept reserved for those more numerate or gifted in mathematics. However, a basic knowledge of probabilities is accessible to everyone and necessary in today's world of rapid change, polarized news, and endless choices. Probability helps us figure out how good are the chances of getting into the program? Is it worth buying insurance for this trip?

Here's a quick guide to probability. A probability of 0 (or a 0 percent chance) means that something won't happen under any conceivable conditions. A probability of 1 (or a 100 percent chance) means that something is certain to happen, no matter what else takes place. Everything else is in-between. For example, an event that's considered very likely might be expressed as 90 percent likely to happen, whereas an event that is unlikely might be expressed as 30 percent likely. This same information also can be expressed as a ratio or frequency: a very likely event is said to occur 9 times out of 10, whereas an unlikely event is said to take place only 3 times out of 10. Or you can use words: weather reports, for example, often use words such as "low" or "medium" in forecasts, for example to communicate "the likelihood it will be raining at 2pm," and connect these to probabilities: a "low" chance of rain at 2pm might be defined as 30 percent or a probability of 0.3, whereas a "medium" chance of rain might be defined as 40–60 percent (a probability of 0.4–0.6).

Most of the time both youth and adults think about uncertainty in terms of descriptive words – we say that a future event is *likely* to happen, or that something *rarely* occurs, or that an outcome is *probable*. And most of the time this is just fine as it gives enough meaning that other people understand what is being said. But when it comes to more consequential decisions, ones that have the potential to significantly affect the life of a young person or those who care about them, it can be helpful to gain additional understanding by linking words to numbers (as in the weather forecasts) or, if more precision is needed, by shifting entirely from words to numbers. This is an important skill, and it's not a hard shift to make, but for many youth it will take some getting used to in order to build up a sufficient comfort level.

> *Serena often stops by the corner grocery store on the way home from her after-school job and buys a bag of chips or a drink. But lately she has been looking at the display of lottery tickets next to the cashier and the brightly coloured announcements of all the money that can be won if you're lucky enough to hold a winning ticket. Serena finds herself wondering if she should start buying tickets regularly and asks her friend Emma if she wants to go in on it with her.*

> *Emma rolls her eyes and makes a scoffing sound. Turns out that Emma has been down this road before. Her mom used to regularly buy lottery tickets. It got so that her mom was spending way too much money and Emma started to notice the impacts on her family. So when her math teacher assigned the class a research project on lotteries, she paid attention. What she found out was pretty alarming: the lottery business brings in nearly $100 billion a year in the US alone, where one in four adults buys a ticket at least once a month. "It's all about decisions and probabilities," Emma tells Serena "and you'll be on the losing side. The pull is that you have a small chance of winning a ton of money, and that small chance of having a multi-million-dollar amount makes you forget about the small probability you'll hold a winning ticket."*

This is another place where the decision mentor has an important role to play, in helping a young person by providing examples or helping them get more comfortable with bringing numeric uncertainty into the picture when they make risky choices. Why use numbers instead of words to describe uncertainty? Two main reasons. The first is that a young decision maker can calculate the uncertainty associated with multi-part events. Consider the simple example of throwing a die and predicting whether the number on top will be even (2, 4, 6) or odd (1, 3, 5). The chance of getting an even number on the first throw is 1 in 2 (50 percent); for both of two throws the probability is 0.5 x 0.5 or 0.25 – only one time out of four, on average, will you see two evens in a row. This is clear information. The second reason is that this insight can now be communicated to others, so they can gain the same understanding. Numbers describe uncertainty clearly, whereas words can easily get cloudy.

Consider this "roll of the dice" example. For the first roll you might say that the chance of seeing an even number is "pretty good," whereas after two throws seeing only even numbers is "unusual" or "unlikely." These vague terms don't encourage clear communication. It's probably not a big deal for our dice example, but suppose you are talking about whether the engine of a used car you're interested in might need an expensive repair, or whether a surgery will work out as you hope? What meaning do you give to someone saying a surgery is "likely" to be successful? Wouldn't a more precise assessment, such as "90 percent of the time – 9 times out of 10 – the operation is successful" make for clearer communication? And if the surgery is only successful 6 times out of 10, wouldn't you like to have access to this more precise information?

Uncertainty is worth paying attention to because it runs throughout the entire decision-making process. Not all sources of uncertainty can be resolved: lots of things that can affect the perceived quality of decisions are subject to natural variation (e.g., the weather, politics) and defy attempts at precise prediction. On the other hand, ambiguity in the language used to describe uncertainty, which affects both facts and values, can often be addressed. Known as *linguistic uncertainty*, it refers to the use of vague terms such as "probable" or "likely" or "usually" that can lead to multiple interpretations and misunderstandings (e.g., if your teenager says he will "probably" be home by 9 p.m., how sure are you – and how sure is he – that this will be true?).

Uncertainty in articulating values can be the result of a novel decision situation or simply sloppy thinking. Uncertainty also can play a role when creating options, especially if their descriptions are left sufficiently ambiguous that different individuals end up interpreting them in different ways. And, of course, when it comes to defining consequences, the available factual information may be quite precise or subject to large degrees of uncertainty: a summer job may pay as little as $12/hour or as much as $20; the decision whether to apply to a post-graduation training program may depend on whether applicants face an acceptance rate of 20 percent or 70 percent.

What can be done, as active decision mentors, to help kids deal with the reality of uncertainty? Recognizing the presence of uncertainty as part of choices, then staying curious and being committed to adapting actions based on what is learned, is harder to put into practice than it sounds. Neither human egos nor brains are always comfortable with acknowledging the influence of uncertainty. Encouraging kids to be as specific as possible, and to make sure that everyone involved in a decision has the same understanding of key sources of uncertainty, is also a helpful reminder.

And if it's hard for an adolescent to proceed with making a decision because of a few key uncertainties, ask what can be done to improve the quality of information – with the benefit of a little time and effort, is it possible to improve the information and then proceed? Finally, it's always good to ask if the uncertainty really makes a difference for the decision at hand. Sometimes the answer is a resounding yes, but at other times even quite imprecise information is all that's needed for a decision maker to move forward responsibly with making a choice.

The reality of acknowledging uncertainty is often humbling for decision makers because humans, of any age, prefer certainty.

Openly dealing with uncertainty and how it influences a decision can build resilience – the ability to prosper no matter how things turn out. As the title of a popular 1990s movie suggests, sometimes "reality bites." Creating resilient options to help deal with uncertainty can provide new decision opportunities and embolden youth for whatever may come.

Lifelong Curiosity

No book can substitute the wisdom gained through first-hand experience. In being curious and learning from their own experiences, a young person can end up with new thoughts and ideas that offer access to better options for creating lives they are excited to lead.

Of course, curiosity has its limits: no matter how much a decision maker learns and how many different perspectives they take into account, the outcomes of many decisions will depend to some extent on luck. Staying curious and seeing decisions as opportunities makes it easier to recognize the appearance of a lucky event. Good luck comes more easily with preparation, and one of the most powerful reasons to be well prepared is to be open to the possibility that good luck will come your way.

A few years ago, the editor of the magazine *Edge* asked leading scientists to report on their favourite equation. Daniel Kahneman, author of *Thinking, Fast and Slow* (2011), contributed the following equations (see Chamorro-Premuzic, 2021):

Success = talent + luck
Great success = a little more talent + a lot more luck

Our ability to control key elements of our lives is far less than we typically assume. This truth doesn't decrease the importance of making good decisions. Even though every once in a while either bad luck or some unexpected external influence will intervene and make things go sideways, it's true that over time a young decision maker will still be better off making higher-quality decisions.

Stay Curious and Adjust: For Your Back Pocket

- Decision makers must be open to receiving feedback so they can modify their decisions in light of what is learned along the way. Being too rigid about a choice or a point of view can lead to outcomes that aren't nearly as good as what's possible if a wider perspective is selected or new information is adopted.
- Pay attention to uncertainty, because it is almost always present and can affect many aspects of the decisions made by youth. Sometimes uncertainty can be resolved, sometimes not – but it's well worth the extra effort to be open about possible sources of uncertainty and to factor these into the decision-making process.
- In part because of uncertainty, we all have less control over the outcomes of our choices than we would like, and generally less than we think we do (remember the earlier discussion of the decision trap "illusory control"?). So it's helpful for a younger decision maker to ask themselves what other influences could affect the outcomes of their choice beyond what comes easily to mind.
- Our lives can be our best teachers. In thinking reflectively about the impacts of their decisions, young people can navigate their futures with increasing agency and intention.

Decision Traps

Representativeness: the failure to see a new person or event in their own light and, instead, slotting or labelling them in terms of other people or events that already are known.

Premature agreement: occurs whenever fatigue sets in or the parties are unable to collaborate and, as a result, decision participants come to an agreement before having done what's needed to arrive at the best possible decision.

Uncertainty neglect: the tendency on the part of many decision makers to ignore or minimize the influence of what is not known.

Practice

For Parents

- Start a conversation about decisions you've made and how you are curious about them and what might have taken place if you'd chosen differently. Reflect on how your choices can provide a window into what you cared about, and why, at a particular time.

- Switch things up: change a routine or tradition – then model curiosity when reflecting on it with your kids. How did it feel to take a different route to school? What was it like eating dinner an hour earlier or later? What else might we do to celebrate birthdays in this family?

- Play a game with your kids in which the task is to assign both verbal and numerical probabilities to facts that are known to others but not to you or your kids. For example, think about the population of Belgium: is it more or less than 15 million people? You can give this a numerical probability ("I'm 80 percent confident it's more than 15 million") and a verbal probability ("I'm pretty sure that … ."). Independently, and without informing each other, the kid(s) you're working with does the same. Then you can check on the factual number and see how well each of you did. At the end of the day, over all the guesses you are making, your numerical probabilities can be checked to see if you are over- or under-confident in your own knowledge level. If you're 80 percent sure of your guesses then 4 out of every 5 times (= to 80/100) your answers should be correct! And it's both fun and insightful to compare your different verbal descriptions; often two people will assign the same numerical probability but use quite different words to describe it. For example, a decision mentor assigns a probability of 30 percent and says something is "unlikely" whereas your kid assigns the same probability of 30 percent but says the event is "likely." A clear case of miscommunication – and a great opportunity for the two of you to get on the same page, before you fail to communicate clearly on a much more important decision.

For Those Who Work with Youth

- Take every opportunity to encourage curiosity in the youth you work with. Beware of overly structuring the problems or assignments you give them, because providing too short a leash can easily dampen a younger person's sense of curiosity.
- Use the Question Formulation Technique (https://rightquestion.org/what-is-the-qft/) to help teenagers brainstorm questions about a topic, using decisions tied to the topic as the core prompt.
- Invite kids to tell or write (or draw or paint!) a story about a decision they have made and why they chose to do what they did.
- If you are a teacher, focus on questions rather than answers. Instead of asking students to answer your questions about a topic, ask them to pose questions.

Go Deeper

- Check out this site from Warren Berger, author of *A More Beautiful Question* (Bloomsbury, 2014), https://amorebeautifulquestion.com. It's loaded with inspiration and ideas for provoking curiosity and finding your own beautiful questions.

- *Getting to Yes* by Roger Fisher, William Ury, and Bruce Patton (3rd ed., Penguin Books, 2011) is a classic book on negotiations, covering techniques and philosophies and with stories throughout describing what to do and what not to do.
- A good summary of the misleading allure of lotteries and people's misunderstandings of uncertainty can be found in the book *For a Dollar and a Dream: State Lotteries in Modern America* by Jonathan Cohen (Oxford University Press, 2022). The histories and stories told by Cohen, although centred in the US, are widely applicable. And a shorter magazine-style version of this perspective, by the journalist Kathryn Shulz, is titled "Scratch That" (*The New Yorker*, October 24, 2022).

Now What?

When Abhay was in grade 10, he made some powerful friendships while on an expedition to the Arctic with the Students on Ice Foundation. Up until then, Abhay had read about how climate change was impacting Canada but had not really experienced it. While in the Arctic he was astonished to see the effects of climate change on nature in real time. He also noted the profound impacts these changes are having on "real people living in the world today ... We could literally hear the ice melting. I kinda felt hopeless at that moment." While he was there, he saw how the ground was shifting, quite literally, under the villages and towns, undermining the lives of his new friends.

After getting home he worried about the fate of his new Inuit friends whose reality meant dealing with the devastating impacts of climate change every day. He reflected upon his experience with his friends and was inspired by their stories of resilience and hope in spite of the harm that climate change has been causing their communities for the past decades. When he texted his Inuit friends, he also learned about the connections between climate change, mental health, and suicide in the North. Suddenly the statistic of Indigenous communities' average suicide rates being eleven times higher than other Canadian communities wasn't just a number. Abhay now felt connected to this horrifying reality.

"Climate change is not just the impact of hurricanes and flooding and other big weather events – it also has vast implications for our health," Abhay says. "I was curious about what might happen if more students from my life back in Southern Canada felt a personal connection with kids up in the Arctic."

Abhay and a team of youth around him decided to start a nonprofit organization called Break The Divide. Abhay opened the first chapter at his own high school. Now there are chapters all over the world. Break The Divide's main goals are to connect youth around the globe, to foster compassion, and to support the actions that this connection inspires.

"Breaking down the socioeconomic, racial, and geographical barriers between communities starts with conversation," says Abhay. "I want to make spaces for those conversations." (Abhay Singh Sachal, personal communication)

Meaningful conversations require skills we develop when making thoughtful decisions. More than a common-sense approach to living, the Decision-Maker Moves enable us to effectively discover and express what matters in ways that get things done. By expanding our scope to include the wellbeing of others, even if the lives of the other people are very unlike our own, we can level up from the personal to the social – from ourselves to family members, to people living in our communities, to our cities and provinces or states, and – in some cases, such as with Abhay – to our world.

Prioritize Teaching and Practising Decision Making

Good decision makers are not born that way. Becoming a good decision maker doesn't require any special genetic inheritance. For better or worse, effective decision making comes through learning some basic skills, practising them, and then paying attention to the lessons you gain through feedback: what works for you and what is confusing, what biases most often trip you up, what outcomes do you routinely forget to include? Becoming a capable decision maker is a lot like learning to cook: it's pretty simple to learn how to fry an egg, but it takes years of practice to become a chef.

Fortunately, the Decision-Maker Moves work well over a wide spectrum of applications, on choices big and small – so that means it's easy to gain lots of experience, with new opportunities for practice arriving every day. On a casual basis, the six Moves organize conversations in ways that emphasize the values and concerns relevant to the decision situation rather than focusing immediately on options. Think of the Decision-Maker Moves as a touchstone that will ground a young decision maker, helping them arrive at a realistic and authentic understanding of possible actions and options. And it's good to start early: teaching the Decision-Maker Moves to children can help them transition from the relative lack of decision-making power of younger children to the world of adult responsibilities.

Kids and Societal Decisions

The common refrain that "our children are our future" needs to be retired. Youth are leaders now. We recognize that favouring youth agency and citizen participation remains a controversial perspective, but perhaps if adult society took youth agency and voice more seriously, we would all be better off.

And today's youth aren't waiting for permission from the adults in their life; they are stepping out on their own, taking a stance on social justice issues like climate change and equity. This proactive stance underscores the need for clear thinking and clear decision making on the part of today's youth and the decision mentors who live and work with them.

Our decisions can be deliberate acts of self-expression. Each decision is an exploration into or communication about who we are, where we belong, and who we are becoming. In developing a deep sense of compassion through relationships with youth in the Arctic, Abhay had the chance to articulate what really matters to him: equity, nature, relationships, understanding, sustainability, and wellbeing. This set of values provides a clear ground on which to stand when making decisions about his life, about what he wants to do with his voice and his time.

Expand the Decision Scope

We began this book by talking about the role of adults as decision mentors, helping the youth in their lives become more capable decision makers. What essential behaviours does this role require?

- listening to the ideas and values of a young person
- providing space and opportunities for them to explore and use their voice
- understanding that the brains of younger and older people are at different points in development and that stages of development impact thinking, both fast and slow, differently
- encouraging and modelling habits that include open-mindedness and scepticism

In a hectic world, it's easy to replace guidelines with rules, suggestions with demands, and two-way conversations with a one-way directive.

To become good decision makers, young people need opportunities to test out ideas and to learn from their decision-making process and the consequences of their choices. The decision mentor has a role to play, ensuring the physical and emotional safety of young decision makers and encouraging them to rely on their own values and preferences, rather than simply accepting suggestions from friends or the internet.

It is also critical that the decision mentor not overstep their bounds. Research by neuroscientists, for example, supports the assumption that providing access to an enlarged scope of decision-making possibilities can actually promote the growth of new neural pathways and circuits in young persons' brains. This means there are neurological as well as behavioural benefits to expanding the scope of decisions a kid is able to make, so that as their environment becomes more expansive, they become more confident and trusting in their own ability to express and to be themselves in the world.

What might this look like? Here are some ideas to get your imagination going. Better yet, look over the following chart with one of the teens you live or work with and see what they might add.

	Decisions youth currently tend to make	Expanded decisions youth could make
Individual	What summer job do I try for?	What would a successful summer look like?
	Do I want a logo on my sweatshirt and, if so, from what company?	What do I need to know about a company's labour and environmental policies before purchasing their products?
	What topic should I choose for my class report?	How can I use my learning to make a difference about big social issues, like climate change or poverty in my community?
	Do I want to try out for a school sports team?	Are there new activities or classes I'd like my school to invest in?
Group	What topic should we do for our class project?	How can we shape school policies and procedures? Or, how should the school board allocate next year's budget?
	What should the theme be for the next school dance?	How can we use our school dance to build community?
	Who will I vote for in our local voting simulation?	What can we do to make sure our voices are heard in the actual election?
	Should our government apologize for historical wrongdoings?	What can we do about our government's historical (and current?) wrongdoings?

Encouraging youth to expand their decision scope also requires a strong dose of reality on the part of the decision mentor. If youth want to contribute to building a new skateboard park in their city or reducing climate change or helping society create stronger protection for LGBTQ2+ kids, it may be unrealistic to think about making much of a difference when acting as an individual (it does happen, but rarely). A decision mentor can be supportive and encourage youth to join forces with others who share the same concerns and passions. This connection to peers and to community gets backs to agency: for some of the bigger issues that affect kids, joining a local, national, or international group can help them contribute to broad-scale desired changes through a combination of their individual and group decisions.

The Urgency of Growing Decision-Skilled Youth

It's one thing for teachers to prepare their students with skills needed to engage in debate; it's another for adults to prepare young citizens to engage meaningfully and compassionately with one another across difference and in collaboration. Politicians typically debate one another, aiming to annihilate their opponents. Nuanced thinking be damned. What might it mean for politicians to engage in a dialogue session where opposing parties assume stances of curiosity and thoughtful, slow thinking? It might not make for good television, but it would make for quite a different world. There is too much at stake to carry on as we have been. We are so connected that

- a virus can shut the global economy down within months
- fires in the Amazon melt Arctic ice
- election results in one country influence whether a species on another continent will survive
- a white policeman kneels on a black man's neck and antiracism demonstrations break out around the world

- the photograph of a dead two-year-old boy on a Mediterranean beach goes viral and tens of millions of people around the world feel a sense of loss and outrage

The decisions we make can impact those we have never met. Today's youth are networked. There is an awareness that yesterday's problems don't need to become tomorrow's emergencies. As a result, many youth have been speaking up and challenging the values by which adults have been making decisions.

In a letter to some United Nations ambassadors, young climate activists wrote the following: "For the young generation who will inherit the consequences of these decisions, it is critical that those who claim to be leading on climate action are held to account for decisions they are making back at home" (Rabson, 2020).

Youth want us to be accountable for our decisions. Our children will, and should, hold us responsible for the decisions we make today. Why did we move to this town rather than that? What did we stand up for when we were young? Why did we decide to do the work we do? Why do we volunteer on behalf of this charity and not those other ones? The thinking underpinned by the Decision-Maker Moves can provide us with good answers.

Learning and using a clear decision-making process provides the teenagers you care about with an accessible way of sorting out their feelings and thoughts. The process sometimes operates fast and intuitively, sometimes slowly and systematically. And it provides a key to youth discovering the connection between their own agency and the choices they make. It helps youth to see through the false assumption that adults are running the world – running their world – according to a rule book. They might not realize we're all just doing the best we can and making it up as we go. Imagine if we all had access to supportive mentors who knew about the Decision-Maker Moves. If we thought deeply about our values and intentionally used them to generate better options. If we routinely distinguished accurate from misleading information. If we remained compassionate and curious about others' perspectives, focused as much on listening as on talking. If we met in dialogue circles rather than at arbitration tables.

Let's support the young people in our lives to sort out what's at play and learn how to make their decisions well. Time to level up and help them go further than we ever could.

You've got this. We all do.

Decision-Maker Moves

1
Frame the decision
What am I really deciding?

2
Clarify what matters
What do I want?

3
Generate options
How can I achieve what I want?

6
Stay curious
What do I need to learn or adjust?

A decision is made

5
Weigh trade-offs
What is best, all things considered?

4
Explore consequences
Would could happen?

Acknowledgments

This book has been inspired by our families, our partners and children and grandchildren, who remind us every day of the very best choices we've ever made in our lives.

Special thanks also go to the colleagues who worked with us on two previous books. *Structured Decision Making* (2012) was written for resource managers and engagement specialists; thanks to Robin's co-authors Lee Failing, Mike Harstone, Graham Long, Tim McDaniels, and Dan Ohlson. *The Decision Playbook* (2019) was written for teachers and is the first place we used the term *Decision-Maker Moves*; many thanks to Robin and Brooke's co-authors Lee Failing and Graham Long.

This book builds on these earlier efforts and the insights and contributions of teachers, school administrators, and colleagues over the past thirty years: it would not exist without the contributions and perseverance of Mark Burgman, Joanne Calder, Tiffany Cherry, Bob Clemen, Claire D'Aoust, Andrew Feldmar, Baruch Fischhoff, Nancy Golden, Terry Gregory, Judy Halbert, Melanie Hall, Gail Higginbottom, Jason Hodgins, Richard Hortness, Nicole Kaechele, Linda Kaser, Ron Lancaster, Joanna Macintosh, Dave Markowitz, Jacob Martens, Kevin O'Connor, Christine Oliver, Margaret O'Reilly, Ralph Keeney, Brett Pierce, Terre Satterfield, Paul Slovic, Scott Slovic, Neil Stephenson, Janet Thompson, Kristen Vogel, and Leisha Wharfield.

Whatever clarity comes through in our writing is due to the inputs of our two patient initial editors. Joanne Wise, enabler of coherent sentences, helped to coach us from ideas to page and taught us about the power of language and precision. Sarah Harvey, our guide to the mysterious world of trade books, did her best to knock the academic language out of this book and respectfully nagged us about fun stuff like formatting, consistency, and the proper deployment of humour. Both of your dedication to this project and the change we hope it inspires lifted us and kept us focused on the goal: thank you. Kathy Kaulbach, miracle illustrator of Touchstone Design House, helped us with visual presentation of the ideas and played a key role in making our message more accessible and, we hope, more fun. The light, insightful touch she brings to our illustrations helped remind us of the common-sense basis of the Decision-Maker Moves and that a good decision-making process can and should be fun.

To our many colleagues who have informed our learning, thank you for your insights and wisdom and for your many critical and challenging questions (even if we weren't always so thrilled at the time). To our friends who encouraged us and kept believing in the power of the Decision-Maker Moves, thank you. We love the stories so many of you shared about taking the Decision-Maker Moves from your offices and classrooms to your living rooms and kitchen tables, using them in your own lives.

And to all the students who have shaped, learned, and used the Decision-Maker Moves: Yahoo! Fantastic! Witnessing you use the Decision-Maker Moves as a way to define who you are while you explore and shape the world has shown us a powerful vision of the future, the one you are creating right now. May the world you leave to your kids be a little bit wiser and more compassionate than what we pass on to you.

Glossary

Anchoring bias: the tendency to settle on a single idea and stick with it even if subsequent information calls for a rethink.

Availability bias: gives too much attention to recent or particularly vivid outcomes – the information that is most readily available.

Confirmation bias: occurs when we look to confirming evidence and ignore contradictory information.

Decision mentor: you! A trusted person who knows the Decision-Maker Moves well enough to guide another person in making a thoughtful decision.

Decision traps: mental shortcuts people young and old take when making a decision, helpful in some situations but also leading to errors that result in less thoughtful decisions.

Endowment effect: the perception that things we see as belonging to us have more value.

False constraints: untested or invalid boundaries and limitations we place on our own decisions.

Groupthink: when people in a group start to take on the ideas seen as agreeable to other members, decreasing overall creativity and breadth of thinking.

Herding behaviour: where everyone simply takes the easiest path and falls into line with the loudest or most persuasive voices in a room or group.

Illusory control: the perception that someone – ourselves or others – has more control over what happens than we or they really do.

Indigenous knowledge system: there is no one definitive Indigenous knowledge system or worldview. However, often Indigenous perspectives on decisions are more holistic and give more weight to spiritual, place-based, multi-generational, and cultural concerns than Western knowledge systems and worldviews.

Indigenous Peoples: also referred to as First Peoples, because they were living on lands well before settlers arrived from Europe or elsewhere.

Linguistic uncertainty: refers to the use of vague terms such as "probable," "likely," or "usually" that can lead to multiple interpretations and misunderstandings of an uncertain event.

Myopia: the tendency to overemphasize short-term considerations to the neglect of longer-term considerations.

Narrative fallacy: occurs whenever people are more attracted to a storyline than to the truth.

Optimism bias: people's tendency to think that their own actions are more likely to result in good outcomes than the averages based on behaviours by everyone else.

Option-focused or alternatives-focused thinking: when people prioritize thinking about options or alternative actions without giving full consideration to the relevant values.

Planning fallacy: a type of decision bias usually associated with being overly optimist about predicting how long it will take to do something.

Premature agreement: occurs when fatigue sets in during a difficult group decision and parties come to an agreement before having done the work to arrive at the best decision.

Prominence bias: occurs when a decision maker oversimplifies a decision and pays attention to only its most prominent or most easily justified aspects.

Psychic numbing: when our response to large numbers is muted because our brains cannot compute things on a mass scale. For instance, we often respond less to a mass casualty event than when we hear about a heart-breaking experience involving one person.

Representativeness bias: the failure to see a new person or event in their own light and, instead, slot or label them in terms of other presumably similar people or events that already are known.

Status quo bias: framing future decisions in a way that encourages the decision maker to stay with what is familiar or habitual and continue to do what has been done before.

Sunk cost bias: errors in thinking that can encourage pursuing a course of action long after our more sensible side tells us it's no longer the right choice.

Uncertainty avoidance: the tendency on the part of many decision makers to ignore or minimize the influence of what is not known.

Value-focused thinking: a phrase coined by Ralph Keeney, referring to an approach for making choices that reflects and addresses what matters to us in this decision context.

Worldview: the ideas and beliefs underlying how individuals build their understanding of the world and their place in it.

References

Aguon, J. (2022). *No Country for Eight-Spot Butterflies*. Astra House.

Bjalkebring, P. & Peters, E. (2020). Aging-related changes in decision making. In *The Aging Consumer: Perspectives from Psychology and Marketing*, ed. A. Drolet & C. Yoon. Routledge.

Bloom, P. (2016). *Against Empathy: The Case for Rational Compassion*. Ecco.

Bond, S. D., Carlson, K. A., & Keeney, R. L. (2010). Improving the generation of decision objectives. *Decision Analysis*, 7(3), 238–255.

Brown, B. (2018). *Dare to Lead*. Random House.

Burgman, M. (2016). *Trusting Judgements: How to Get the Best out of Experts*. Cambridge University Press.

Carr, D. (2016). Why young people should care about aging. *Psychology Today*. www.psychologytoday.com/gb/blog/the-third-age/201609

Carter, C. (2020). *The New Adolescence*. BenBella Books.

Chamorro-Premuzic, T. (2021). Talent, effort or luck: Which matters more for career success? *Forbes*, September 27.

Chrona, J. (2022). *Wayi Wah! Indigenous Pedagogies: An Act for Reconciliation and Anti-racist Education*. Portage and Main Press.

Damour, L. (2017). *Untangled: Guiding Teenage Girls Through the Seven Transitions into Adulthood*. Ballantine Books.

Dillard, A. (1999). *For the Time Being*. Alfred A. Knopf.

Duke, A. (2018). *Thinking in Bets: Making Smarter Decisions When You Don't Have All the Facts*. Penguin Books.

Failing, L., Gregory, R., Long, G., & Moore, B. (2019). *The Decision Playbook: Making Thoughtful Choices in a Complex World*. GutsNHeads Project.

Fischhoff, B. (1996). The real world: What good is it? *Organizational Behavior and Human Decision Processes*, 65(3), 232–248.

Fischhoff, B. (2008). Assessing adolescent decision-making competence. *Developmental Review*, 28(1), 12–28.

Fischhoff, B. & Kadvany, J. (2011). *Risk: A Very Short Introduction*. Oxford University Press.

Fischhoff, B., Lichtenstein, S., Slovic, P., Derby, S., & Keeney, R. (1981). *Acceptable Risk*. Cambridge University Press.

Fisher, R., Ury, W., & Patton, B. (2011). *Getting to Yes* (3rd ed.). Penguin Books.

Franklin, B. (1772/1975). *The Papers of Benjamin Franklin*, vol. XIX, *January 1 through December 31, 1772*, ed. William B. Willcox. Yale University Press.

Gallo, A. (April 28, 2010). You've made a mistake. Now what? *Harvard Business Review*. https://hbr.org/2010/04/youve-made-a-mistake-now-what

Gregory, R., Failing, L., Harstone, M., Long, G., McDaniels, T., & Ohlson, D. (2012). *Structured Decision Making: A Practical Guide to Environmental Management Choices*. Wiley-Blackwell.

Halbert, J. & Kaser, L. (2022). *Leading through Spirals of Inquiry: For Equity and Quality*. Portage and Main Press.

Hammond, J., Keeney, R., & Raiffa, H. (1999). *Smart Choices: A Practical Guide to Making Better Decisions*. Harvard Business School Press.

Hoggan, J., with Litwin, G. (2016). *I'm Right and You're an Idiot: The Toxic State of Public Discourse and How to Clean It Up*. New Society Publishers.

Hsee, C. K. (1996). The evaluability hypothesis: An explanation for preference reversals between joint and separate evaluations of alternatives. *Organizational Behavior and Human Decision Processes*, *67*(3), 247–257.

Huber, G., Payne, J., & Puto, C. (1982). Adding asymetrically dominated alternatives: Violations of regularity and the similarity hypothesis. *Journal of Consumer Research*, *9*, 90–98.

Joseph, B. & Joseph, C. F. (2019). *Indigenous Relations: Insights, Tips, & Suggestions to Make Reconciliation a Reality*. Indigenous Relations Press.

Kahneman, D. (2011). *Thinking, Fast and Slow*. Doubleday.

Kahneman, D., Sibony, O., & Sunstein, C. (2021). *Noise: A Flaw in Human Judgment*. Little, Brown Spark.

Kahneman, D. & Tversky, A. (1979). Prospect theory: An analysis of decision under risk. *Econometrica*, *47*, 263–291.

Kahneman, D. & Tversky, A. (1984). Choices, values, and frames. *American Psychologist*, *39*(4), 341–350.

Keeney, R. (1992). *Value-Focused Thinking: A Path to Creative Decisionmaking*. Harvard University Press.

Keeney, R. (2020). *Give Yourself a Nudge*. Cambridge University Press.

Knetsch, J. (1989). The endowment effect and evidence of nonreversible indifference curves. *The American Economic Review*, *79*, 1277–1284.

Levine, T. R. (2014). Truth-Default Theory (TDT): A theory of human deception and deception detection. *Journal of Language and Social Psychology*, *3*(4), 1–15.

Lichtenstein, S. & Slovic, P. (2006). *The Construction of Preference*. Cambridge University Press.

Lord, C., Ross, L., & Lepper, M. (1979). Biased assimilation and attitude polarization: The effects of prior theories on subsequently considered evidence. *Journal of Personality and Social Psychology*, *37*(11), 2098–2109.

McNeil, B. J., Pauker, S. G., Sox, H. C., & Tversky, A. (1982). On the elicitation of preference for alternative therapies. *New England Journal of Medicine*, *306*(21), 1259–1262.

Nutt, P. (2004). Expanding the search for alternatives during strategic decision making. *Academy of Management Executives*, *18*, 13–28.

Olson, D. & Windish, D. (2010). Communication discrepancies between physicians and hospitalized patients. *Archives of Internal Medicine*, *170*(15), 1302–1307.

Payne J., Bettman, J., & Johnson, E. (1992). Behavioral decision research: A constructive processing perspective. *Annual Review of Psychology*, *43*, 87–131.

Pink, D. (2009). *Drive: The Surprising Truth about What Motivates Us*. Riverhead Books.

Qu, Y., Fuligni, A., Galvan, A., & Telzer, E. (2015). Buffering effect of positive parent–child relationships on adolescent risk taking: A longitudinal neuroimaging investigation. *Developmental Cognitive Neuroscience*, *15*, 26–34.

Rabson, M. (2020). The Canadian Press. Posted June 10, 2020. www.cbc.ca/news/politics/greta-thunberg-canada-un-1.5605830

Rebanks, J. (2015). *The Shepherd's Life: Modern Dispatches from an Ancient Landscape*. Doubleday Canada.

Shanteau, J. (1992). Competence in experts: The role of task characteristics. *Organizational Behavior and Human Decision Processes*, *53*(2), 252–266.

Siegel, D. & Bryson, T. (2012). *The Whole-Brain Child*. Bantam Books.

Sinek, S. (2011). *Start with Why: How Great Leaders Inspire Everyone to Take Action*. Portfolio.

Slovic, P., Finucane, M., Peters, E., & MacGregor, D. (2007). The affect heuristic. *European Journal of Operational Research*, *177*, 1333–1352.

Slovic, P., Västfjäll, D., Erlandsson, A., & Gregory, R. (2017). Iconic photographs and the ebb and flow of empathic response to humanitarian disasters. *PNAS, 114*, 640–644. doi: 10.1073/pnas.1613977114

Slovic, S. & Slovic, P. (eds.). (2015). *Numbers and Nerves: Information, Emotion, and Meaning in a World of Data*. Oregon State University Press.

Stephens, B. (2017). The dying art of disagreement. *New York Times* (opinion), September 24.

Wheelan, C. (2012). *Naked Statistics: Stripping the Dread from the Data*. Penguin Random House.

Yeager, D., Dahl, R., & Dweck, C. (2018). Why interventions to influence adolescent behavior often fail but could succeed. *Perspectives on Psychological Science, 13*, 101–122.

Online Resources

An interview with Paul Slovic about ideas from the book *Numbers and Nerves* can be seen on the Arithmetic of Compassion website: www.arithmeticofcompassion.org/blog/2021/2/15/a-morning-show-interview-with-paul-slovic

If you don't have time to read Kahneman's impressive book *Thinking, Fast and Slow*, check out the quick summaries on YouTube:

www.youtube.com/watch?v=9ivtvPVkFkw (two-minute summary); www.youtube.com/watch?v=uqXVAo7dVRU (ten-minute summary)

Index